iT (l 6/88) New 7/88
4/94 16c
3/00 1 LAD
7/05

The Philippine State
and the Marcos Regime

Cornell Studies in Political Economy

EDITED BY PETER J. KATZENSTEIN

Power, Purpose, and Collective Choice: Economic Strategy in Socialist States, edited by Ellen Comisso and Laura D'Andrea Tyson

The Political Economy of East Asian Industrialism, edited by Frederic C. Deyo

Politics in Hard Times: Comparative Responses to International Economic Crises, by Peter Gourevitch

Closing the Gold Window: Domestic Politics and the End of Bretton Woods, by Joanne Gowa

The Philippine State and the Marcos Regime: The Politics of Export, by Gary Hawes

Pipeline Politics: The Complex Political Economy of East-West Energy Trade, by Bruce W. Jentleson

The Politics of International Debt, edited by Miles Kahler

Corporatism and Change: Austria, Switzerland, and the Politics of Industry, by Peter J. Katzenstein

Small States in World Markets: Industrial Policy in Europe, by Peter J. Katzenstein

The Sovereign Entrepreneur: Oil Policies in Advanced and Less Developed Capitalist Countries, by Merrie Gilbert Klapp

International Regimes, edited by Stephen D. Krasner

Europe and the New Technologies, edited by Margaret Sharp

Europe's Industries: Public and Private Strategies for Change, edited by Geoffrey Shepherd, François Duchêne, and Christopher Saunders

National Styles of Regulation: Environmental Policy in Great Britain and the United States, by David Vogel

Governments, Markets, and Growth: Financial Systems and the Politics of Industrial Change, by John Zysman

American Industry in International Competition: Government Policies and Corporate Strategies, edited by John Zysman and Laura Tyson

The Philippine State and the Marcos Regime

THE POLITICS OF EXPORT

GARY HAWES

382.4109

CORNELL UNIVERSITY PRESS

Ithaca and London

6/88

First published 1987 by Cornell University Press.

International Standard Book Number 0-8014-2012-1
Library of Congress Catalog Card Number 86-29237
Printed in the United States of America
Librarians: Library of Congress cataloging information appears on the last page of the book.

The paper in this book is acid-free and meets the guidelines for permanence and durability of the Committee on Production Guidelines for Book Longevity of the Council on Library Resources.

Contents

Preface

In 1986 the Philippine people were rightfully proud of the example they had set for the rest of the world. Through "people power" they had ousted Ferdinand Marcos, and their expectations for social and economic change were running high. With a commission sitting to write a new constitution, there was also widespread hope for permanent political change.

I first went to the Philippines in July 1972, also a time when prospects for political change were high. Even an outsider, a newcomer to the Philippine political scene, could sense then that an old social and political order was in decline. A constitutional convention was in session; political opposition, both violent and nonviolent, was commonplace; peasants, workers, and intellectuals were all organizing and becoming involved in the political debates of the day.

The nature of political change was dramatically altered later that same year with the declaration of martial law. Initially, people hoped that martial law would bring a new sense of discipline and direction to the nation and its economic development. Bureaucratic reforms, the collection of thousands of loose firearms, and rapid economic growth made many optimistic.

I worked in Manila for the next two years for the Department of Agriculture of the Republic of the Philippines, and from a position within the bureaucracy and from my job-related travels it was easy enough to see the results of the policies of President Marcos. The

7

early years of the Marcos regime were devoted to political consolidation and economic development based on increased exports.
The regime pursued these two goals—greater political control and
increased exports—despite their effects on land ownership patterns, standards of living, respect for human rights, the nation's
ecology, or almost any other measure for quality of life one might
choose to adopt.

Agriculture, I was convinced, and especially export agriculture,
was central to the nation's history and its future. But how did
agricultural exports mesh with the international economy? How
did the demands of the international economy, in turn, shape domestic politics and economics? And what was the significance of the
new, more intrusive role the state was playing in the economy? In
1980 I returned to research some of these larger concerns of political economy.

The agricultural sector has long shaped the Philippine political
system. The enormous wealth generated over the years by the
coconut, sugar, and fruit products industries, coupled with the
huge numbers of workers employed in them, had made industry
leaders important political actors. Every Philippine president had
been drawn from these industries or had been forced to develop
political coalitions based on support from them. By 1980, however,
things had changed. The Marcos government had become strong
enough to take over the trading of sugar from a once-powerful
sugar bloc; it was clearly in the midst of taking over the trading and
processing of coconuts.

These takeovers were targeted at potential domestic challengers
to the president, but they also led the Philippine government to
take actions that raise questions about the nation's traditional role
in the world economy. Here was a Third World country, deep in
debt, forcing out such foreign investors as the giant U.S.-based
grain trader Cargill and the Mitsubishi Corporation of Japan—
hardly the actions of a weak and dependent government. The
agricultural export industries, I believed, promised insight not only
into the workings of the Philippine political system but also into the
role of the nation in the world economy. A book about the Philippines from the perspective of political economy thus may have
important lessons for our understanding of other developing nations. This book also documents a mechanism central to the long

dictatorship and extraordinary theft of the Marcos regime—control of the lucrative agricultural industries. The political corruption and national economic collapse presided over by Marcos are problems that continue today despite his flight to the safety of a hideaway in Hawaii. This book, therefore, also has long-term implications, many of them somber, for the prospects of the young regime of Corazon Aquino and the vibrant democracy she leads.

Chapter 1 provides a more detailed introduction to the theoretical concerns of this book and places the agricultural export industries in their historical, political, and economic contexts.

Chapters 2, 3, and 4 are devoted to the coconut, sugar, and fruit products industries respectively. The findings are based on both secondary sources and a wide variety of interviews. I conducted interviews with government officials, members of political parties (both the official government party and opposition parties), representatives of Filipino and foreign investors in each of the three industries, political activists (both those above ground and those working underground), and the people who actually produce and process these agricultural exports—workers, farmers, and their family members, who continue to live in poverty despite the wealth that these industries generate. Where discretion is necessary, these interviewees have been kept anonymous.

The narrative returns in Chapter 5 to the larger issues of regime and state. I use my findings from the case studies to develop a broader understanding of the Philippines and of the role that the Philippines plays in the current international political economy.

I hope that this book provides a helpful perspective for explaining the interrelated and long-standing political, economic, and military crises through which the Philippine people have suffered in the first half of the 1980s. The research on which it is based was originally funded by the East-West Center in Honolulu, Hawaii. While in the Philippines I was a visiting research associate of the Institute of Philippine Culture of Ateneo de Manila University. My thinking has benefited from interaction and feedback from colleagues too numerous to name at the Third World Studies Center of the University of the Philippines, the Departments of Political Science at the University of Hawaii and the University of Michigan, the Center for South and Southeast Asian Studies at the University of Michigan, and the East-West Center. My deepest debt of gratitude is to Jovito Salonga, former Philippine senator and current minister of the Presidential Commission on Good Government. His assistance opened many doors for me in the Philippines, and our long discussions during his exile in Hawaii were always enjoyable and educational.

The manuscript has benefited from reviews by two anonymous readers at Cornell University Press and the detailed suggestions made by Peter Katzenstein, editor of Cornell Studies in Political Economy.

I conclude this work with a deep sense of gratitude to all those who have assisted me and a fervent hope that the newly won political freedoms in the Philippines and the national sense of optimism are not just temporary. But more than this, I hope that political freedom and optimism can be translated into a better life for the small farmers, the workers, and their families who produce so much of the nation's wealth in the form of agricultural exports.

GARY HAWES

Ann Arbor, Michigan,
and Manila, Republic of the Philippines

The Philippine State
and the Marcos Regime

CHAPTER ONE

Creation of the Philippine Political Economy

In 1986 the twenty-year rule of one of Asia's most astute politicians, one of the strongest of the strong men, came abruptly to an end as Ferdinand Marcos fled the Philippines. His departure brought the Philippines a great sense of relief and of hope for the future. Fourteen years earlier most Filipinos had known a similar sense of relief and hope; on September 22, 1972, President Marcos had placed the entire Philippines under martial law. The trend toward political chaos had ended, it seemed then as it seemed in 1986, and a new era of national discipline and economic development was about to begin.

In Proclamation Number 1081 declaring martial law, Marcos had argued that the security of the nation was under threat from a growing leftist movement determined to overthrow the government, a threat compounded by worsening Muslim-Christian conflict in the southern Philippines.[1] Using his power as commander-in-chief of the armed forces, Marcos closed the Philippine Congress; he subordinated the judiciary to the executive by demanding signed, undated letters of resignation from all judges; and he engineered the ratification, by show of hands in open assemblies, of a new constitution that allowed him to remain in office indefinitely.

Marcos, in short, had staged an internal coup. He had overthrown a working, two-party democratic system of government modeled after that of the United States. He had centered political power in the executive branch, and the presidency was in his tight grasp.

In the early years of martial law his personal power was at its height, and so was the strength of the Philippine state. The military and civilian bureaucrats who administered the martial law regime were, for the first time, somewhat insulated from the demands of civil society. Emergency constitutional provisions gave those in control of the state the authority and the military power to vanquish alternative political leaders and to punish segments of the bourgeoisie opposed to the new model of development—export-oriented industrialization. Most surprisingly, the state even forced several important foreign corporations out of their lucrative positions in the Philippine economy, replacing them with what at the time were alleged to be private, locally owned companies that were to spearhead a new drive toward development.

Marcos skillfully wove together a broad political coalition that was loyal to him personally. He used military repression and legal harassment against those who opposed him, and he financed his martial law government with vastly increased foreign loans, foreign aid, and new investments from abroad. Much of this capital, newly invested in the Philippines, was attracted because the Marcos regime had the imprimatur of the World Bank, the International Monetary Fund, and the U.S. government.[2] The Marcos coalition thus included the vast majority of foreign investors, their local partners, the business community linked by political interest to the president, local politicians who remained in office because of their allegiance to Marcos, and the military officers who enforced martial rule. It was a strong coalition, firmly commited to order and discipline, poised to lead the Philippines down a new path to development.

But authoritarian rule came to an end. The final days before the flight of Ferdinand Marcos on February 25, 1986, are glorious days in the history of the Filipino people, whose courage and principle will serve as an example to others struggling against dictators. During the three days that culminated in February 25 many of Marcos's troops deserted, those who remained loyal would not (or could not) fulfill orders, millions of civilians defied the president's orders and surged into the streets to protest and to practice peaceful civil disobedience. After almost fourteen years of harsh political repression the dictator was banished, carried into exile with friends, loot, and family in the airplanes of his staunchest international backer—the government of the United States.

How could Marcos, the modern authoritarian, the man who sought to re-create the East Asian economic miracles of South Korea, Taiwan, and Singapore, have failed so miserably? He seems in retrospect to have resembled more the weakened and fallen dictators of Brazil, Argentina, and Peru than his East Asian contemporaries. Clearly, integral parts of his coalition had deserted him and defected to the side of his challenger, Corazon Aquino. Military units would no longer follow orders that Marcos issued from the isolation of the presidential palace. The business community refused to invest in a moribund economy corrupted by the president and his cronies. And in the final crisis Marcos's international backers—the IMF, the World Bank, and the U.S. government—refused to come to the rescue yet again, deciding that Marcos had finally outlived his usefulness.

Marcos fell so dramatically for reasons that combine politics and economics. The turn to authoritarianism in 1972 was clearly linked to the transition to a new path to development—export-oriented industrialization—and this new path required a new political coalition. The transition followed generations of dependence on agricultural exports and a short-lived and unsatisfactory attempt at import-substitution industrialization; it involved a structural change that authoritarianism made possible. But that authoritarianism also allowed Ferdinand Marcos to remain in power for another fourteen years, and so we need not only an analysis that links politics to economics but also one that accounts for the personal motivation of the man, his family, and friends.

The new president, Corazon Aquino, proclaims that her victory was a victory for "people's power." The nature of her ruling coalition we can use to clarify what has happened and will happen in the Philippines. People's power seems to be an expression of the people's demand for an end to the Marcos dictatorship, a yearning for the redemocratization of the nation, and an unwillingness to accept any longer the mismanagement and corruption of the economy by Marcos and his cronies. Beyond that, however, the political and economic content of the Revolution (as it is now called in the Philippines) is not clear. The ruling coalition appears to be diverse and, because of its internal contradictions, unstable. Members of Aquino's cabinet range from conservative, militaristic landlords to moderate leftists who favor dramatic structural changes in the economy; economic advisers range from those who favor a selective repudiation of the nation's international debts to those who feel that Marcos was not faithful enough in following the IMF model of development; some are nationalists favoring a neutral foreign policy, others want to maintain close ties with the United States, including massive U.S. military bases on Philippine soil; many are vehement anticommunists, but others favor compromise and negotiation to welcome back those who under the leadership of the Communist Party of the Philippines took up arms against Marcos.

To understand the rise and collapse of the Marcos regime requires us, I believe, to clarify the important economic bases for political changes that took place during his regime. Only then will it be possible to identify what is truly significant about the Aquino government above and beyond the new president's obvious and deeply felt commitment to redemocratization and her respect for human rights.

If the declaration of martial law was directly associated with the transition to a new model of development, then the collapse of the Marcos regime and the rise of Corazon Aquino may mark a new turning point in the Philippine struggle to develop. It certainly means that the Philippines offers potential insight into the pitfalls of authoritarianism and the pitfalls of an export-oriented path to development. The attempt to sort out the economic, political, and personal causes for the rise and collapse of the Marcos regime will benefit from an effort to place the Philippines in comparative perspective, to see where the experience of the Philippines differs from that of other nations which have chosen a similar path to development.

There will be differences, but there will be many similarities to explore as well, for the Philippines under Marcos shared several characteristics with the newly industrializing countries (NICs) of East Asia and Latin America. The authoritarian rulers of these countries have argued that national discipline and strong centralized leadership are essential to the project of economic development. Marcos, too, used these arguments to rationalize his long tenure in office and to try to push the nation in the direction of export-oriented industrialization. Martial law became a mechanism to implement both personal political goals and more structural, economic goals. Marcos used his powers under martial law, for example, both to attack old political enemies and to depoliticize large segments of Philippine society. The new constitution legit-imized a continuation of Marcos's rule and new policies to attract foreign investment in manufacturing for export, and this confla-tion of the president's personal political goals with the nation's need for economic change is a constant of the authoritarian era after 1972. Its implications for the ability of the nation to achieve economic goals are a subject for detailed analysis in later chapters.

Although the Philippines is in some ways typical of other NICs, however, it is also distinctive, because it has in large part failed in its effort to make the transition to export-oriented growth. Burgeon-ing international debts and protectionism in developed countries have forced flexibility and innovation among the other NICs; they have overwhelmed the Philippines. The manufacturing sector of the economy has stalled, and the overall growth of the gross na-tional product has been negative, declining by about 5.5 percent in 1984 and about 3.5 percent in 1985. As the Philippines has failed where other nations have had at least marginal success, its recent experience should be enlightening about development policy. What is there about the Philippines, its political coalitions, its histo-ry, the sequencing of its industrialization, or its integration into the world market which explains the country's failure to make the transition to export-oriented industrialization, its failure to keep pace with the NICs? This introductory chapter suggests several factors and turning points that seem to set the Philippines apart from other nations (Brazil, Mexico, South Korea) that started the post–World War II era in similar situations but that have since far surpassed the Philippines in levels of industrialization and income.

The Philippines was once the showcase of democracy in the Pa-cific. It was also one of the Third World's wealthiest and most admired members. Under Marcos, though, its recent history has been an almost unbroken record of squandered economic oppor-tunities, growing inequality, and political privilege for one man, his family, and friends. My focus is not Marcos the man so much as what happened under Marcos, what happened under one modern authoritarian who sought first to remain in power and second to lead his nation to industrial growth and national development. In the move to promote industrial growth, new policies were imple-mented, some groups benefited and many more lost out, political coalitions formed and dissolved, new relations were forged with

the outside world, new linkages made to the international economy. Ferdinand Marcos has been an important actor in the drama of
Philippine political and economic development, but he is not the
only actor. I aim to look at the underlying patterns of economic
and political change which led to the rise of Marcos and to the
collapse of his rule; to look at the broad patterns of the integration
of the Philippines into the world economy; and to look at the
distribution of costs and benefits which resulted from fourteen
years of authoritarian rule. To do so, I focus on one sector of the
economy—the agroexport sector—in order to draw out the lessons
both for the authoritarian rule of Marcos and for the attempt to
transform the Philippines into the next Asian economic miracle.

THE PHILIPPINES IN HISTORICAL AND
COMPARATIVE PERSPECTIVE

Any attempt to place the Philippines in comparative perspective
is plagued by a problem pointed out by Stephan Haggard in a
recent review article: there has not been much effort to analyze the
domestic political basis within newly industrializing countries for
various paths to industrialization. Haggard suggests that two sets of
questions are important: "First, what domestic political factors account for the different development trajectories of the East Asian
and Latin American NICs?" Equally important in explaining specific policy reforms is the "political independence of state elites
from societal actors," since "state autonomy is crucial in accounting
for turning points, such as the shift to export-led growth, when
incentives are restructured and a new growth coalition is forged.
Without autonomy or insulation from the demands of particular
social groups, the pursuit of policies such as land reform, lowering
of real wages, raising of interest rates, devaluation, or lifting of
subsidies or protection would be impossible."[3] Domestic political
factors and elite independence both guide my analysis in this book.
They focus attention on issues that are of central importance—
models of development, differences in the political coalitions that
support alternative models of development, the timing of industrialization, the adaptation of domestic entrepreneurs and the domestic economy to the international environment, and the distribu-

tion of costs and benefits within particular models of development.

These matters concern what happens inside the Philippines; we have to modify our understanding of them to take into account the Northeast Asian political economy. Bruce Cumings argues that the foundations of present-day development in the region were laid in the colonial era, with the Japanese occupation of Korea and Taiwan and with the integration of these colonial economies into a larger sphere of economic domination.[4] The political economy of the present-day Philippines, like that of Taiwan or of South Korea, is a product of many factors, but especially important is the way in which the colonial experience shaped class and economic structures.

What we need, then, is an analysis that identifies factors for cross-national comparison but at the same time takes into account the specificity of the Philippine historical experience. I emphasize three broad historical trends or turning points. These must be understood if we are to establish the domestic political factors that account for the development trajectory of the Philippines and the political independence of state elites. All are related to the nation's elite: the emergence of a landholding elite, the diversification of the elite after World War II, and the breakdown of elite cohesion in the 1960s.

These changes in the nature of the elite are all related to broader patterns of economic development. During the colonial era (after the opening of the Philippine economy by the Spanish) the concept of economic development was linked to the expansion and diversification of agricultural exports, and the political system grafted on to this economic base during the twentieth century was modeled after U.S. democracy. The landholding elite firmly controlled both the economy and the polity. The state elite was virtually identical with the economic elite, and so the state was not insulated from civil society. In fact, it was thoroughly penetrated, rendering any discussion of alternative paths to development futile.

It was not until the destruction of the Philippine economy during World War II and the imminent bankruptcy of the nation's treasury immediately afterward that import and exchange controls were imposed. They led indirectly to a decade-long experiment with import-substitution industrialization (ISI). ISI resulted in a diversification of the Philippine social structure as foreign investors sought joint-venture partners and middle-class managers. Domestic capital was transferred out of the agricultural and into the industrial sector, and with industrialization came greater urbanization and more workers in the modern sector of the economy.

This postwar rise in production of manufactured goods for the domestic market created the conditions for a similar rise in political conflict. New questions arose about what degree of foreign control of the economy was acceptable, the degree to which domestic entrepreneurs ought to be protected, the proper exchange rate for the peso, who should bear the burdens of taxation to finance industrialization, and a host of other contentious issues.

The state, of course, was not insulated from these demands and debates within the larger civil society. In fact, the government itself was often divided between supporters of agricultural and export-led growth, on the one hand, and supporters of a more nationalist, populist path to development based on further ISI, on the other.[5] The result was indecisiveness and economic stagnation. As a consequence the Philippines started the transition to export-oriented industrialization almost a decade later than the Asian NICs.

Marcos broke the policy stalemate in 1972; his declaration of martial law resolved the breakdown in elite cohesion in favor of the export sector. Martial law freed the state from penetration by the demands of civil society. State elites suddenly acquired the freedom, without fear of internal opposition, to open the economy and reintegrate the Philippines into the world economy as an export platform.

The creation of a landed elite, the diversification of that elite, and the breakdown of elite cohesion have profoundly affected the political economy of the Philippines. They have affected important domestic political conflicts and thus determine the selection and timing of sequences of industrialization. In the more detailed historical discussion that follows, I show both how coalitions within the elite have determined the path of Philippine development and how the Philippine experience has differed from that of Taiwan, South Korea, and Brazil.

Emergence of a Landholding Elite

The Philippines has long been one of the world's largest exporters of tropical agricultural products. Members of the landholding elite have been major earners of foreign currency, significant employers of rural labor, and owners of the nation's richest resources. Historically they have played a pivotal role in Philippine politics.

Landholding in the Philippines first became important as a source of wealth and prestige in the late 1700s, when the Spanish colony began to export agricultural crops. Following liberal reforms in the 1790s Spain and the Spanish colonial administration in the Philippines began to open the economy to new, more dynamic commercial forces. In 1790 the port of Manila was opened to vessels flying foreign colors. In 1814 residence and trading rights were granted to foreign firms. In 1823 the Spanish Cortes allowed foreign business firms to set up offices in Manila, and in 1829 foreigners were given permission to enter Manila on the same footing as Spanish traders.

This opening of the Philippines to foreign merchant houses brought dramatic changes to the colony. Conservative, mercantilist policies had linked the Philippines almost exclusively to Spain; when these fetters were removed, vastly expanded markets became available, stimulating a rapid growth in the production and export of indigo, sugar, and "Manila hemp" (abacá). The merchant houses, primarily English and American, served as conduits bringing new production, processing, and transportation techniques to old commodities, and they also implemented a system of credit advances to producers (often against their better commercial judgment and against the wishes of their superiors) which further stimulated the supply of agricultural commodities for export.[6]

The advent of large-scale agricultural exports made land a source of prestige and tremendous wealth. Leslie Bauzon has argued that "the realization that land itself could be a source of wealth, that land had economic value, dawned largely upon the Spaniards, the *mestizos* (persons of mixed parentage), and the upper-class Filipinos. . . ."[7]

There was an element of ethnic diversity among members of the landholding elite, as Bauzon indicates. Spanish administrators, missionaries, soldiers, and settlers, always few in number, were outnumbered by Chinese artisans and traders. The Chinese had been trading in the Philippines before the Spanish arrived, and their number and economic role expanded under Spanish rule. Indeed, until 1768 Spanish civilians had been prohibited from living in the provinces, largely at the instigation of the religious orders, which wanted to concentrate on converting the natives (then called *indios* by the Spaniards).

The number of Chinese and Spanish landholders was quite small, at least until the commercial economy had become more fully developed later in the 1800s. Most land was held by a group known collectively as the *principalia*: primarily the leading indio families and mestizos, most often offspring of the union of Chinese fathers and indio mothers.[8]

Patterns of land acquisition were quite varied. Many of the Spanish landholders were given royal land grants. Similarly, many of the principalia, who served important administrative roles in the indirect style of Spanish colonialism, received royal grants of land for their loyalty or service. But there were numerous other ways the less powerful or less scrupulous could get land. Increasingly the wealthy and powerful accumulated land through both legal and illegal means.[9]

The religious orders were also large landholders. These orders, serving as missionaries, had received royal land grants and had over time greatly expanded their estates by purchase, by land grabbing, and by generous gifts of land received from pious Spaniards and members of the principalia. At the end of the nineteenth century, it is estimated, clerical estates totaled over half a million acres in the provinces near Manila.[10]

The latter half of the nineteenth century saw the acceleration of trends begun in earlier decades. The opening of the Suez Canal and improvements in agricultural production and processing technology, along with increased prices and demand for Philippine goods, especially sugar, led to rapidly growing exports. In 1855 sugar exports totalled 53,000 tons and abacá 12,000 tons. By 1895 (the nineteenth century's peak year for exports) sugar exports were 376,000 tons and abacá exports were 107,000 tons.[11]

Increased exports produced increased wealth for the landholding elite. Regardless of their ethnic background, the wealthier landholders began to adopt a more "European" lifestyle. They sent their children to school and to university, occasionally even to Europe for advanced training, and Spanish became their common language. Their houses and possessions reflected their wealth, and in an important way this helped to link the Philippines to the world market—the importation of expensive consumer goods made the

Philippines far less self-sufficient in economical terms. Many elite landholding families became the economic equals of the Spanish colonialists, and some members of these families began to receive training in law, medicine, and the priesthood.[12]

From this common economic background, lifestyle, and outlook, the indio elite, the mestizos, and some locally born Spaniards began to develop a common identity. They began to see themselves as Filipinos.[13] They shared not only an identity but also a set of grievances. Their sons in the priesthood, for example, suffered discrimination at the hands of the Spanish church hierarchy. Also, administrative positions in the colonial government were reserved for *peninsulares* (Spaniards born in Spain), though such newcomers were usually less wealthy and less well educated than the local agrarian elite. After the Latin American revolutions of the early 1800s, many Spanish administrators from the former colonies migrated to the Philippines, creating an even more oppressive and overstaffed bureaucracy. Although Filipinos gradually gained access to prestigious political and bureaucratic positions during the second half of the nineteenth century, they were always under Spanish superiors.

Some Filipinos—especially the well-educated, known as *ilustrados*—began to agitate later in the century for liberal reforms in the colonial administration and, ultimately, for representation in the Spanish Cortes on an equal footing with the citizens of Spain itself. These political demands define the ilustrados as an elite, and the connection between status and political demand is a recurring theme in Philippine political economy. The Filipino landholding elite has a privileged economic position, and as it rests on economic inequality, its political goals must, first and foremost, not threaten its economic advantage. In the late 1800s it was politically progressive for ilustrados to demand reforms, representation in the Cortes, or independence for the Philippines. The elite, however, was not interested in self-liquidation, and so its members did not seek radical transformations in Philippine society. They were politically progressive but economically conservative. And their progressiveness extended only so far as it did not threaten their economic position. This ambivalence of the agrarian elite would first appear during the Philippine Revolution and the Philippine-American War, but it shows up again and again in subsequent Philippine history.

The revolution against Spain had many causes—the oppressive and rigid bureaucracy, lack of political liberties and avenues for local participation, growing agrarian unrest on the religious estates around Manila, and the execution of popular leaders such as Fathers Gomez, Burgos, and Zamora in 1872 and José Rizal in 1896. The leadership of the revolution was initially in the hands of urban artisans and workers, along with small landholders and tenants from the religious estates around Manila, but eventually leadership passed into the hands of the ilustrados. Under their leadership there was less emphasis on land seizures and radical transformation of society and greater emphasis on liberal reform, moderate change, and compromise with first the Spanish and later the Americans.

The landholding elite of the province of Pampanga was probably typical of the landholding elite as a whole. John Larkin tells us that this elite

> reacted to each phase of the revolution according to their own self-interest and need for survival. At times their interest coincided with the aims of a broader Philippine nationalism and at times not. Pampanga's leaders, though in favor of moderate reform of the Spanish colonial regime, backed down on the issue of complete independence. Yet once the Spaniards were eliminated from contention, a native government loomed as the best alternative. Finally, when Aguinaldo's government failed to hold the country, Pampanga accepted the stability offered by the Americans. . . .
>
> The landlords belonged to a conservative tradition that looked to stable government for the preservation of their property.[14]

American Rule

The Spanish-American War brought U.S. naval forces to the Philippines, and in 1898 Admiral Dewey defeated the Spanish Navy in Manila Bay. By this time the revolutionary army of the Filipinos had already bottled up most Spanish troops in Manila. President McKinley ordered American troops sent to the Philippines in early summer of 1898. By the time the Treaty of Paris ending the Spanish-American War was signed on December 10, 1898, Washington had made the decision to keep the entire Philippines.

The Filipinos did not accept American claims of ownership, and fighting broke out in February 1899 between troops of the United States and the newly created Philippine Republic. It took almost three years for the U.S. military to reduce the fighting to sporadic guerrilla encounters and to gain firm military control of the islands. In sum, from 1898 until the Japanese invaded fhe Philippines in December 1941 and again, briefly, from liberation to independence on July 4, 1946, the United States held colonial power in the Philippines.

American rule, after the brutality of the Philippine-American War, was comparatively enlightened. Little money was spent on the colonial bureaucracy, because possession of the colony was to be only temporary, or on a colonial army, and so, Theodore Friend notes, "Concomitantly, the amount of money the Philippine budget allotted for 'social services'—for education and health—was higher as a proportion of total expenditure than in British Malaya or French Indo-China and nearly three times greater than in the Netherlands East Indies."[15] Significant advances were made under American rule in education, health, communications, transportation, and some sectors of the economy.

American rule, for our analytical purposes, had two major impacts. The first was the development of free trade relations between the United States and the Philippines. The second was the evolution of a democratic system of government dominated by the landholding elite.

The United States—with the consent of the Filipino socioeconomic elite—tied the Philippine economy to the U.S. economy by means of tariff policy. Under the Payne-Aldrich Tariff Act and the Philippine Tariff Act, both passed in 1909, American goods shipped directly were permitted to enter the Philippines duty free without limitations as to volume and foreign material content. Philippine products, except sugar and tobacco products, which were subject to fixed annual quotas, were permitted to enter the United States free of duty.

The Underwood-Simmons Tariff Act of 1913, which governed commercial relations until 1934, removed all remaining quota limitations and export duties. These new tariffs were largely effective in cutting off Philippine trade with countries other than the United States. By 1930, 63 percent of Philippine imports came from the

United States and 79 percent of Philippine exports went there. The linkage of the Philippine economy to that of the United States had important commercial and political effects. In the words of Friend,

> Reciprocal free trade drastically limited Philippine ability to protect native manufacturing and radically stimulated a taste for American consumer goods. Money which might have gone, in a more austere culture, into capital investment, instead went into luxuries and prestige purchasing. The importing habits of the Filipinos would make economic independence always difficult to obtain, and their exporting habits even weaken the desire for political independence. Concentrating as they did on profitable agricultural exports, especially sugar, coconut oil, and hemp, and relying as they did on American buyers, many Filipino investors began to grow wary of independence unless it could be connected with continued free trade.[16]

American economic policy toward the Philippines was dominated by the assumption that free trade would allow the principle of comparative advantage to work its developmental magic. Guaranteed free trade also made the Philippines an attractive area for American investment, and it was during this colonial period that Del Monte made its first Philippine investment in pineapples, Hawaiian investors began to follow their counterparts on the U.S. mainland by investing in the Philippine sugar industry, and smaller investments were made by U.S. companies and individuals in cordage, coconuts, and rubber.

Free trade, of course, had its opponents—primarily among vegetable oil and sugar producers in the United States and nationalists in the Philippines who favored more rapid independence with greater national control of the economy. At the time, though, a transnational coalition of importers of Philippine raw materials, exporters in the Philippines and the United States who benefited from free trade, and U.S. investors in the Philippines combined to control decolonization and the negotiations over economic relations between the two countries after independence.

One reason it was possible to assemble any transnational coalition in support of peaceful, gradual decolonization and continued close economic ties to the United States was the American policy of democratization in the colony. The policy was, in its turn, successful because it did nothing to threaten the economic interests of the transnational coalition. In fact, the transnational coalition supervised the entire process.

Creation of civilian governments by way of municipal elections had begun as soon as possible, and local elections were held in some areas as early as 1901. In 1907 the first elections for national office were held, and by 1916 legislative control of the colony was completely in the hands of Filipinos. These early politicians and the people who elected them were a very select group. Describing the politics of the early 1900s, Carl Landé notes that "at first, property and literacy requirements continued to restrict the franchise to essentially the same small elite from which had been drawn the principales of Spanish times, and the pattern of politics changed little. In each town families which had fought one another for pueblo offices in Spanish times continued to compete for what were now called municipal offices."[17]

It was from this existing elite, from among the ilustrados and provincial landholding politicians, that the United States recruited its allies. "If the ilustrados had not existed," as Norman Owen says, "it would have been necessary for the Americans to invent them. . . . By 1899 the United States was already looking for Filipino leaders with whom a *modus vivendi* could be arranged, a means of saving not only the costs of repression and local administration, but also what was left of her ideals and self-image."[18]

Though the United States did not invent the ilustrados, it certainly had representatives capable of recruiting members of the Philippine elite for active cooperation and where possible providing support to see that they were elected to high office.[19]

The basis of cooperation between representatives of the United States and elected Filipino leaders was free trade, continued reliance on both U.S. investments and agricultural exports for economic growth, and a gradual transition to complete Philippine control of the government. Ultimately the Philippines would be granted independence. A Commonwealth government was inaugurated in 1935 with Manuel Quezon as president, and on July 4, 1946, despite the devastation of World War II, the Philippines became independent.

At the time of independence Philippine political and economic systems were firmly in the hands of a landholding, agricultural elite generated by Spanish and American colonial policies. This elite was

27

extremely wealthy because it produced and exported agricultural commodities to the protected U.S. market. It had solidified its social status by sending its sons and daughters to prestigious universities in the Philippines and abroad for training as doctors, lawyers, and other white-collar professions. Indeed, though based on agricultural exports, the elite was gradually becoming more diversified. It was not until well after World War II, however, that the rural elite began to lose its tight grip on power.

The Philippine elite survived World War II intact and retained political power.[20] The economy, however, was devastated, and there was an immediate need for rehabilitation and relief. The United States responded in 1946 with the Tydings Rehabilitation Act, which committed $620 million for reconstruction. Unfortunately for the Philippines, however, the U.S. Congress tied the disbursement of funds under the Act to the requirement that no amount in excess of five hundred dollars be given for any single claim unless and until an agreement had been reached by the presidents of the United States and the Philippines regarding trade relations between the two countries. This executive agreement, which required an amendment of the constitution of the newly independent Philippines, was justified on the grounds that it would speed the rehabilitation of the agroexport economy of the Philippines. It is, this justification notwithstanding, a splendid example of neocolonialism.

The agreement included six main provisions:

1) a system of duty-free as well as absolute quotas was instituted for Philippine products, such as sugar and tobacco, which competed with American products.

2) Philippine commodities not covered by quotas and all American commodities were to be free of duty from July 4, 1946 until July 3, 1954 (subsequently extended to December 31, 1955). Tariff rates were to be raised 5 percent per year beginning in 1955 until they reached full duty status in 1974.

3) The exchange rate of the Philippine peso was tied to the U.S. dollar at a rate of two to one, and there were to be no restrictions on the transfer of funds from the Philippines to the United States except with the agreement of the U.S. president.

4) Perhaps most important was the provision of "parity rights" to U.S. citizens.

The disposition, exploitation, development, and utilization of all agricultural, timber and mineral lands of the public domain, waters, coal, petroleum, and other mineral oils, all forces and sources of potential energy, and other natural resources of the Philippines, and the operation of public utilities, shall, if open to any person, be open to citizens of the United States and to all forms of business enterprise owned or controlled, directly or indirectly, by United States citizens.[21]

5) The U.S. president was given discretionary power to withdraw any or all of the substantial economic concessions granted to the Philippines if there was any indication that nationalistic pressures were being applied against U.S. interests. This power was never used. It did, however, serve as an effective deterrent of nationalist action against the United States.[22]

6) The Philippines was prevented from imposing export taxes. Until the Revised Trade Act became effective in 1956, this clause prevented the use of a weapon that, in the words of one economic study, "could have been effective both for protection against uneconomic terms of trade losses, and also for the transfer of some income from traditional exports to other sectors. The latter was especially important in the case of sugar, which enjoyed a price premium in the protected U.S. market." The loss of this weapon was extremely costly: "alternative means of squeezing export income were much inferior because they cut across-the-board among all sectors, including manufactured exports."[23]

These provisions were all included in the Philippine Trade Act of 1946, also known as the Bell Trade Act. Inherent in the Act was the assumption that the quickest path to recovery for the Philippines was the reinstitution of free trade, leading to broader access to the U.S. market for Philippine agricultural exports. The Act also assumed that guarantees to U.S. investors were necessary to step up the flow of American capital that would finance the rebuilding of Philippine manufacturing facilities.

The Philippine Trade Act, together with the effects of the colonial years, served to strengthen those sectors of the economy involved in the production and initial processing of primary products. Landowners earned high profits during this era under an elite-dominated, weak central government whose very ability to channel the profits of export agriculture to areas of the economy where they would have benefited larger segments of the populace was circumscribed by the trade act. These provisions represented at the very least a severe compromise of Philippine independence. At worst they provided for structural distortions in the Philippine economy which exist to this day.

The experience of the Philippines with its Spanish and American colonial masters lends dramatic support to the argument that Bruce Cumings advances regarding Taiwan and South Korea. Cumings asserts that "if there has been a miracle in East Asia, it has not occurred just since 1960; it would be profoundly ahistorical to think that it did. Furthermore, it is misleading to assess the industrialization pattern in any one of these countries: such an approach misses, through a fallacy of disaggregation, the fundamental unity and integrity of the *regional* effort in this century."[24] In the colonial experience of the Philippines we see a similar linkage between the Spanish and American colonial administrations, on the one hand, and the evolution of the Philippine social structure and choice of development models, on the other. The status of the Philippines today as a dependent agricultural exporter in large part reflects earlier colonial policy.

In contrast, Cumings tells us, both Taiwan and South Korea benefited from a decision by Japan in the 1930s largely to withdraw from the world system and pursue a self-reliant, go-it-alone path to development. By the mid-1930s these two colonies were becoming receptacles for industries such as iron and steel, chemical, and electrical generation. Speaking of Taiwan alone, Alice Amsden concurs.

> In the 1930s, Japan reshaped its policy of transforming Taiwan into a source of food supply for the home market. The shift in policy can be understood only in the context of Japan's increasing militarism and expansionism in the Pacific. Belatedly and frantically, Japan sought to refashion Taiwan as an industrial adjunct to its own war preparations. . . . From a few industries with strong locational advantages before 1930 (e.g., sugar and cement), industry in Taiwan expanded in the 1930s to include the beginnings of chemical and metallurgical sectors, and as World War II cut off the flow of duty-free goods, some import substitution began.[25]

It seems clear that on one crucial point, the timing of the start of industrialization, colonialism is a key factor. Spanish and American

Indeed, in the period leading up to the final collapse of the Marcos government, it was clear that U.S. security concerns limited Washington's ability to distance itself from Marcos and play a more constructive role.[28] In the entire postwar era more generally, U.S. security interests seem to have become gradually paramount as U.S. economic interests in Southeast Asia have diversified away from the Philippines.

It was economic factors, however, that first began to break down the tight collaboration which had characterized U.S.-Philippine relations. Economic crisis forced the Philippine government and the elite that dominated it to implement policies they would never have accepted in normal circumstances. By the late 1940s the Philippines began to suffer from growing balance-of-payments deficits—caused by declines in U.S. government spending in the Philippines, declining prices for agricultural exports, and increasing imports of consumer goods. The government responded by imposing import controls in 1949 and exchange controls in 1950. These policies, plus a high tariff enacted in 1957, resulted in a period of import-substitution industrialization that lasted for more than a decade.

The major beneficiaries of the government's development policies during the 1950s and early 1960s, Robert Baldwin argues, were "those who own[ed] or control[led] business in the industrial sector. Exchange control as well as related import-substitution policies created enormous windfall gains and profit opportunities in the industrial sector, which were then exploited by a vigorous Philippine entrepreneurial group."[29] It must be emphasized, however, that these Philippine entrepreneurs were joined by a rapidly growing number of foreign investors—primarily American and protected by parity rights. The World Bank has also calculated that there was a major shift in the internal terms of trade away from agricultural and toward nonagricultural goods during the decade of the 1950s.[30]

The imposition of exchange and import controls during the 1950s set in motion certain changes in the Philippine political economy and accelerated other trends whose results became apparent sometimes only years later. Among the most significant were a rise in nationalism, a growing centralization of political power in the executive branch, and a diversification of the economic interests of the political elite. These three trends represent the social forces that, when coupled with the personal ambitions of Ferdinand and Imelda Marcos, would result in the declaration of martial law in 1972.

Import and exchange controls, along with protective tariffs, were the major policy tools in the development of import-substituting industries in the Philippines, just as they were elsewhere in the developing world. Much of the technology, managerial know-how, and capital for these new industries was provided by multinational corporations. The multinationals, however, also needed local partners who could arrange licenses, labor, and local plant facilities.

The growth of new industries producing for the domestic market had two important impacts. First, in the United States the economic interest group relating to the Philippines was no longer limited to the importers of Philippine agricultural and mineral products and the exporters of consumer goods to the Philippines. In the 1950s, for the first time, American investors in the Philippine market had concerns other than the simple maintenance of free trade. Their concern was now to accelerate economic development, leading to an enlarged domestic market. Second, the Philippine elite no longer spoke with one voice on economic and commercial policy. Agricultural exporters favored low wages, free trade, and limited government interference in the economy. Import-substituting industrialists, on the other hand, tended to favor higher wages (certainly within very strict limits, and primarily to enlarge the domestic market), economic growth, restrictions on free trade, and an active government that fostered domestic industrialization. To be sure, these differences between exporters and import-substituting industrialists were muted because often they occurred within single families that had interests in both sectors of the economy. Yet differences over policy implementation did develop and were an important source of political conflict during the 1950s and 1960s.[31]

Import and exchange controls also heralded a new era in which the power of the central government would dramatically increase. Previously the key to political harmony and economic stability had been a government that protected the favored position of Philippine exporters to the U.S. market. Now the advent of controls gave the government an even greater capacity to control the direction of the economy and to make or break individual entrepreneurs. The government controlled the licensing of new import-substitution ventures, the granting of import permits, the right to exchange pesos for the dollars needed to import, and the amount of hard currency exporters got after turning in their export receipts to the Central Bank. So the government had greater economic power; but when it tried to use that power, it did so almost always in response to demands from one or another segment of the bourgeoisie, usually that segment with the best political connections. The result was constant political conflict, charges of corruption and favoritism, and the failure to respond dynamically, as a *national* economy, to changes in the international economic environment.

In terms of domestic politics, not only was the central government strengthened during the 1950s and 1960s, but within the central government, the executive branch gained power at the expense of the legislature. The president had always controlled the release of government funds, but with an increased role for economic planners, the new emphasis on technical expertise in the control of the economy, growing economic and military assistance from abroad, and an ever-greater resort to foreign borrowing to supplement locally available capital for investment, the power of the executive branch grew. For the first time, it even began to extend into the countryside, into the smallest political units of the nation.[32]

Increased political participation followed World War II, and its consequence was a need to mobilize ever greater numbers of voters. There also emerged a new group of professional politicians at the local and provincial level. Their appearance meant some power was transferred, Kit Machado has argued from the traditional landholding political faction leader—dependent on his own resources and thus relatively independent of the national political leadership—to the new professional politician who depended on funding from the national party to mobilize voters at the local level. The development enhanced national power at the expense of local power.[33]

The 1950s and 1960s were also a period of rising nationalism, a nationalism that stemmed in large part from the realization that national sovereignty meant little without national control of the economy. Filipinos increasingly found it offensive that much of the commercial and financial sectors was in the hands of the Chinese minority and that foreign investors or multinational corporations controlled large parts of the mining, industrial, and manufacturing sectors. Economic nationalism initially took the form of Filipiniza-tion of imports (by controlling import licensing) and retail trade (by act of Congress).[34] Official government support for industrializa-tion by Filipinos also grew, and it peaked under the "Filipino First" policies of President Carlos P. Garcia (1957–61). Later in the 1960s, nationalism became less a tool the government used to gain control of the economy, more an organizing tool of those who opposed the government and favored a radical restructuring of society. Nationalist outrage came to focus on the parity rights given to Americans just after World War II, the U.S. military bases in the Philippines and the use of those bases in support of the war in Vietnam, the domination of the economy by multinationals, and the perceived subservience of national economic planning to the dictates of the World Bank and the International Monetary Fund.

Breakdown of Elite Cohesion

Elite cohesion broke down during the 1960s, as several scholars have noted, and this breakdown also contributed to the declaration of martial law. Jonathon Fast argues that "until the late 1960s the Philippine oligarchy had been remarkable in its homogeneity as a class. . . . By the beginning of Marcos' second term [1970], howev-er, oligarchic unity had begun to crumble and this was expressed in growing personal mistrust of Marcos." Jeffrey Race says that "what has happened since 1972 represents a historic fracture in the co-herence of the Philippine ruling groups." David Wurfel argues that "Filipino elite cohesion helped produce a period of political sta-bility for twenty-six years after independence, consistent with the expectations of the conventional political science wisdom. That sta-bility was nevertheless disrupted by the intensity of interfactional struggle despite that cohesion."[35]

What terminated the elite cohesion that had characterized Phil-ippine society after independence? The growing power of a group of import-substituting industrialists was, as suggested above, im-portant in the breakdown. Also the influx of foreign investors—first to jump the protectionist barriers erected in the 1950s and later to take advantage of the effects of a 1962 devaluation of the peso—made elite cohesion more difficult to maintain. The 1962 devaluation was the result of a stabilization agreement with the International Monetary Fund; another agreement was necessary in 1970. These agreements hurt the working class and the protected ISI sector of the economy most of all. Likewise, the Investment Incentives Act of 1967 (Republic Act 5186) and the Export Incentives Act of 1970 (Republic Act 6135) further opened the economy to foreign investors at the expense of domestic investors.

The strength of family ties and the small size and homogeneity of the elite were no longer sufficient to maintain cohesiveness. Now too many important actors participating in the economy were not Filipino—the IMF, the World Bank, and the multinationals, among others. The struggle to determine the direction in which the Philippine economy would go became increasingly divisive. One segment, broadly nationalist in character, favored protection for domestically owned industry and curbs on foreign investment. The more radical elements within this segment, with support from students, workers, and intellectuals, agitated for an end to U.S. bases in the Philippines and an end to domination of the economic policy-making process by the International Monetary Fund. The other segment of the elite favored a rapid end to government protection of local industry coupled with new support for agricultural exports, policies to attract foreign investors, and a foreign policy closely tied to the United States.

President Marcos, because of his attempts to open the economy, attract foreign investors, and work with the IMF and World Bank group, was widely believed to be firmly in the camp of the elite segment favoring an open economy.

The conflict within the elite opened the floodgates of popular political participation by peasants, workers, students, and intellectuals. They championed a range of nationalist and structural reforms. Under steady attack the Marcos administration (indeed, the entire political system) began to suffer a loss of legitimacy.

Reflecting popular pressure for reform and the loss of governmental legitimacy were two major events in the early 1970s. In response to insistent calls for reform, the government had allowed elections to choose representatives to a new constitutional convention. This convention sat in 1972 and had, according to draft provisions circulating at the time, instituted changes that, if ratified,

37

would have radically altered the groundrules for foreign investment; they would also have prevented Marcos from running for office again after his second term of office ended in 1973.[36] Second, the Supreme Court responded to public opinion by issuing rulings that limited the rights of Americans in the Philippine economy.

The potential for revolutionary change in the early 1970s should not be overestimated. It does seem clear, though, that important elements of the elite were under concerted attack. For a growing number of Filipinos, neither the political system nor the continued domination of society by a small elite was legitimate. Technocrats, foreign investors, agricultural exporters, and, most especially, Marcos himself saw that the privileged positions they had occupied during the 1960s were threatened. The political sphere had been enlarged to incorporate new social forces, including the politically important nationalists, students, and workers, and for the first time, elite domination of Philippine society was in doubt.

The sequence of industrialization by import substitution with a broadening of the political spectrum in support of a strengthening of the domestic market is typical of South America, especially of Argentina as analyzed by Guillermo O'Donnell. In the Philippines, as in several Latin American countries, economic stagnation, political conflict, and a rising left resulted in a political crisis. From that crisis emerged an authoritarian government determined to pursue a new path to development.

South Korea and Taiwan passed through an import-substituting phase that was, by comparison, much shorter. This phase, as Cumings says,

> did not have the political characteristics it had in Brazil and elsewhere. Politics did not stretch to include workers, peasants, or plural competition for power. The political sequence of inclusion followed by exclusion, as the 'easy' phase ended and export-led development began, was absent. Labor was excluded in the 1950s and remained excluded in the 1960s; nor did the squeezed middle class of bureaucrats and small businessmen achieve representation in either Taiwan or South Korea.[37]

In two important ways, then, the Philippine transition to export-oriented development differed from that in Taiwan and South Korea. First, the political sphere was much broader in the Philippines during the import-substituting phase. This was so not just domestically but also in the sense that international investors had stronger links to local capitalists and through them more influence in shaping the local path to development. Second, because the political sphere was broader in the Philippines, the state had less relative autonomy. The transition to export-led development, in consequence, involved greater conflict.

Exports were made profitable in Taiwan and South Korea and the protection of production for the local market was largely removed in the early 1960s. Of Taiwan in this period Amsden says, "not only were exporters wined on tax and credit subsidies; they also dined on tariff reductions from pre-war China heights. This allowed them to take advantage simultaneously of advanced levels of world productivity for their inputs and exotic Taiwan wage levels for their outputs."[38] Both states implemented similar packages of monetary, fiscal, tax, and trade policies. Most important, they devalued currencies and reduced tariff protection; foreign investment was attracted and free trade zones were established. These packages of new policies brought results, for by the mid-1960s both South Korea and Taiwan were embarked on the road to industrialization for export.

A third and final point of difference concerns the timing of industrialization. The Philippines devalued its currency in 1962 but failed significantly to reform the tariff policy that protected import substitution until many years after the declaration of martial law. New foreign investment was sought during the 1960s, but most of it went into the agricultural export sector, not into new manufacturing for export. The power of the import-substitution sector of the economy was curbed, but there was no easy transition to export-oriented industrialization. In this the Philippines was again more like Latin America than Taiwan and South Korea: it went through a decade of economic stagnation and political conflict, the 1960s, before it made a sharp break with the past with the declaration of martial law.

Martial Law

Within the first few months of martial law massive changes were made in the Philippine political economy. Nationalistic rulings by the Supreme Court were severely restricted in their implementation or contradicted by presidential decrees. The draft constitution then being deliberated posed a critical challenge both to foreign investors and to the continued rule of Marcos; it was swept away by threats, bribes, and the intimidation of delegates to the constitutional convention, and the final draft of the new constitution contained no ban on the continuation in office by Marcos. The president strengthened his hand against the landholding elite that dominated provincial politics by closing Congress, a bastion of support for the agricultural exporters, and by implementing a limited program of land reform in rice and corn lands. The power and scope of the executive branch expanded substantially, and, perhaps most important, the military got bigger, its role in maintaining civil order and opportunities to participate directly and indirectly in the economy were all vastly enhanced, and soldiers' pay was increased.

Economic incentives shifted dramatically in favor of exporters and foreign investors. Throughout the 1970s new incentives were added to attract foreign investment, while at the same time tariffs were liberalized and subsidies to producers for the local market were reduced. As part of a shift to development based on export-oriented industrialization, wages were repressed and the power of unions to organize, bargain collectively, and to strike was sharply curtailed. The political sphere, which had expanded in the 1960s, now contracted with the strict implementation of exclusionary policies.

The IMF and World Bank group seldom issues an unequivocal backing of the policies of any Third World country. In 1976, however, it said with respect to the Philippines that

> toward the end of the 1960s the government became aware of the shortcomings of past development policies and since the early 1970s [i.e., after the imposition of martial law] it has been introducing economic reforms in an effort to correct past deficiencies and broaden the base of the population in the development process. More emphasis has been given to agriculture and rural development, to export promotion, to public infrastructure, and to employment creation. There is little question that the Philippines has the physical and human resources required for sustained economic improvement during the next few decades and its more equitable distribution. Moreover, the recent economic and social reforms have contributed to a policy environment more conducive to sustained economic growth.[39]

Foreign investors shared the judgment of the World Bank. Total foreign investment approved by the Philippine Board of Investment in 1971 was roughly 150 million pesos, and 300 million pesos in 1972. In the first full year of martial law foreign investment reached 538 million pesos, and in 1974 it was 1.4 billion pesos.[40] What began to emerge in the early years of martial law, therefore, was a triple alliance of multinational, state, and local capital (similar to what Evans describes in Brazil) rather than a clearly dominant state that controlled the local and multinational capital, as in South Korea and Taiwan.

With Congress closed and the Supreme Court subservient to the executive, domestic politics was radically different after 1972. The power of local politicians to control followers, to develop their own political machines, became largely superfluous because there were no elections to participate in. The president, moreover, no longer needed local support for his own election. He now depended on his power as commander-in-chief of the armed forces to remain in office, and votes were no longer a valuable commodity. In fact, the country went through a process of depoliticization—elections were not held, civil liberties were restricted, mass political meetings were prohibited, many opposition leaders were imprisoned, and those who persisted in their political activities were often charged under nebulously defined laws against subversion.

The authoritarian politics of the Philippines under Ferdinand Marcos was in many ways similar to those of the other newly industrializing countries. Yet Marcos's politics was built on a foundation that is uniquely Filipino. The actions of Marcos were not just in response to a changing international economy or to class conflict within the Philippines. Acting to protect his own interest, he was acting within a specific political culture. A few of the patterns of that political culture must be illustrated before we return to more comparative themes.

UNDERSTANDING PHILIPPINE POLITICS
AFTER MARTIAL LAW

Philippine politics under authoritarian rule bore little resemblance to the years before martial law, when a stable, elite politics was based on regular alternation of officeholding between two very similar political parties. These parties were pyramidal arrangements of political factions tied together by patron-client ties. Indeed, as Kit Machado has noted, "pre–martial law studies of parties and elections are of little use as a base for cumulating further knowledge about current political processes." These studies suffered a "widespread failure to identify what proved to be the vulnerability of democratic institutions to a centrally directed coup," a failure he traces to the fact that most studies in the 1960s used a "democratic development framework within which research was designed and findings interpreted."[41]

Within that democratic development framework one of the most influential works on Philippine politics is Carl Landé's *Leaders, Factions, and Parties*. It describes a two-party system in which the parties are almost identical, are dominated by elites at all levels, and where national parties are little more than alliances of provincial, municipal, and local-level factions. Landè, like most political scientists writing in the 1960s, was optimistic that the Philippine political system was stable. He believed that the pattern was unlikely to change "as long as the little people in most parts of the country continue to accept as a matter of course the political leadership of their patrons among the big people of their respective communities. So long, that is to say, as political organization continues to be structured by vertical dyads of patronship and clientship rather than by a categorical sense of common interest based on region, industry, and class."[42]

Jean Grossholtz argued that the system before 1972 was, in fact, even more democratic than it seemed on the surface, because of traditional Filipino bargaining. Such behavior guaranteed that political power would be used to provide rewards to followers. As Machado summarizes the pre-1972 model,

> political activities were intensely competitive, and this competition was expressed largely through a two-party system in reasonably fair elections that regularly resulted in orderly transfers of power. The parties, dominated by shifting alliances of elite factions, did not differ in any significant way. They reached deeply into rural society and were held together by traditional social ties, patronage, and pork barrel. Political behavior was largely governed by such features of Philippine life as the primacy of kinship and *compadrazgo* (ritual kinship) and the importance of reciprocity in social interactions.[43]

The leaders of the elite factions were most often landowners. As Landé points out, "a large proportion of municipal and provincial leaders, if not also of barrio leaders, even those engaged in the professions such as the law and medicine, are members of the landowning gentry."[44] This elite had the economic and political resources to resist controls from the national level. The political system immediately after World War II Landé portrays as dominated by a group of rural officials and politicians whose economic base was in landholding and who controlled local and regional politics. It was not until Marcos declared martial law that a Philippine president was able to assert national, executive-branch control over local factions led by the landowning elite.

The success of Ferdinand Marcos in usurping democracy and presiding over a turn to authoritarianism which lasted for fourteen years dictates that we think about Philippine politics in new ways. But if we cannot rely on the democratic development framework provided by the modernization school of social science, where are we to turn for models to help us understand politics in the Philippines since martial law? There are, I believe, two areas of research which provide helpful insights. One is a small body of research conducted in the Philippines in the late 1960s and early 1970s, which gave some indication of what was to come. The other is comparative: we must begin looking for lessons from authoritarian polities in other parts of the Third World.

Field research in the late 1960s and early 1970s began to suggest that significant changes were taking place in Philippine politics. As the spoils of victory increased, so national elections were becoming more intense. The greatly enhanced economic role of the government made control of the central organs of governance vital. The greater intensity of elections, along with the expansion of suffrage, resulted in greater mobilization and, as Machado argues, in many areas of the country the political leadership of the old leading families was overthrown by professional, career politicians.[45]

The decline of the traditional rural politician began, Thomas Nowak and Kay Snyder explain, with the desire to accumulate surplus more effectively and to shift capital into the profitable early stages of industrialization. Patrons reduced their obligations to clients wherever they could. As these authors argue, "when a free enterprise system is imposed on a feudal social structure and bonds between patron and clients weaken, inequality is likely to increase since the restraints on the increased expropriation of surplus by patrons are lessened."[46] Growing inequality was, in turn, important in stripping the system of legitimacy during the 1960s.

Although the decline of rural patrons brought on a polarizing effect, the replacement of patrons by political machines led by professionals can be viewed as a positive trend. Machado says that "while a democratic pattern of political development was still being pursued, the emergence of professional politicians and local machines could be viewed as steps en route to a more viable party system." And as Nowak and Snyder note, "if sufficient resources are allowed to move from the center to the local areas, political machines should prove capable of integrating and mobilizing large groups of people."[47] As we now know, of course, political machines did not develop smoothly. The Philippine political system broke down when rural patrons were abdicating their traditional roles, when competition within the elite was at its greatest, and when political participation (in a variety of forms) was threatening the legitimacy of the political system.

It may be possible, however, to find explanations of these Philippine phenomena elsewhere. As we have already seen, events in the Philippines share some characteristics of a pattern relatively common among Third World countries that have undergone import-substitution industrialization.

In Latin America the modernization school held early expectations that greater economic and social equality and more democratic forms of politics would emerge from economic growth. Those expectations proved illusory there just as in the Philippines the expectation of stable two-party democracy was dashed by martial law. In response to the rise of a "new" authoritarianism in Latin America scholars examined the relationship between economic change, particularly industrialization, and the emergence of regimes that they characterized as both bureaucratic and authoritarian. Among the original contributors to this debate was Guillermo O'Donnell, who argued for a connection between the end of the easy phase of import substitution and the emergence of authoritarian regimes. Import-substitution industrialization at some point reaches a stage when all the easily manufactured consumer goods are already being produced locally behind protective tariff barriers. Then it is common for the perception to develop (especially among Western-trained technocrats) that further economic expansion will have to be based on large-scale, capital-intensive investment in producer goods industries. Lack of local capital means that the transition to this new phase depends on foreign investors or foreign loans. The easy phase of ISI was built on nationalist, populist, and participatory policies. With the new stage of ISI came new needs, however: needs for long-term stability and predictability, for the financial austerity that lenders often require and for the labor discipline necessary to attract foreign investors. All of these needs run counter to the preceding political environment. Democratic governments cannot contain the tensions created by the perceived necessity for sharp departures from previous policies and cannot resolve the stalemate that often develops when separate factions of the elite support different policies for development.[48] The makeup of the ruling political coalition, its relative strength, and the relative autonomy of the state elites thus all determine the smoothness with which a country makes the transition from one phase of industrialization to the next.

O'Donnell's thesis, though not universally accepted, seems to be applicable to the Philippines.[49] The decade of the 1960s was characterized by growing recognition that the easy phase of ISI was over, and an often acrimonious debate over what policies should be followed to restore rapid economic growth broke out. Political participation was no longer limited to voting at election time; demonstrations, strikes, and riots became commonplace as the public increasingly involved itself in policy debates. The executive branch of the government, with its economic planning offices dominated by technocrats, was leading the nation toward a more open economy in which foreign capital would play a larger role. The legislative and judicial branches were more responsive to nationalist, populist pressures, both from the public and from certain segments of the import-substituting industrial bourgeoisie. The declaration of martial law broke the policy stalemate. However, that declaration benefited one person more than any other—President Ferdinand Marcos. By choosing to declare martial law, Marcos cleared the way for a concerted effort to shift the nation to the path of export-led industrialization. At the same time he enhanced his own role in the political system, which allowed him to reward his loyal friends and family.

Agroexport Industries and the
Study of Philippine Politics

The following chapters are concerned with the impact that the authoritarianism brought on by the declaration of martial law—the breaking of the policy stalemate—had on various agricultural export industries. I am concerned with the rise of new export industries and new investments in old industries; the change in the distribution of costs and benefits within industries; and the impact of the continued, massive export of agricultural products from a country where today two serious problems are growing rural landlessness and growing levels of malnutrition.

For a study of the Philippine political economy which seeks to place the Philippines in comparative perspective—one which is interested in explaining the rise and the collapse of the authoritarian rule of Ferdinand Marcos—there is no better place than the agricultural export sector on which to focus our attention. Since at least the eighteenth century the export of agricultural products has been central to the Philippine political economy; the export of tobacco, indigo, abacá, sugar, and coconut products was the basis for the integration of the Philippines into the U.S. economy. Agricultural exports generated tremendous wealth, which produced a landholding elite that dominated local and provincial politics under the Spanish and, later, assumed important roles in the struggle for independence from colonial rulers, both Spanish and American.

In 1935 the United States promised independence to the Philippines. The promise came from negotiations between the U.S. government and a Philippine leadership whose political and economic power was based in the agricultural sector and which was most responsive to the interests of the agricultural exporters. After World War II the political system of the independent Philippines remained dominated by agricultural exporters. This domination was only to be expected, because the Philippine economy was extremely dependent on the export of agricultural products. If we use 1970 as an example, the ten leading exports from the Philippines that year, in descending order of total value, were: logs, sugar, copper concentrates, coconut oil, copra (the dried meat of the coconut), canned pineapple, plywood, desiccated coconut, copra meal/cake, and lumber.[50]

But the importance of the agricultural export sector is not just economic, I believe, it is also political. In the 1970s the coconut industry employed or provided an income for roughly 20 percent of the nation's entire population. The sugar industry, while smaller, still was the main source of livelihood for approximately nine out of every hundred Filipinos. These are important blocs of voters. In combination, then, the wealth generated by the agricultural export industries, coupled with a sizable population base, made the leaders of the coconut and sugar industries into important political actors.

That Marcos regarded these industries as vital he made abundantly clear, by taking over both sugar and coconuts after the declaration of martial law. These takeovers were intriguing because they were not just targeted at potential challengers to Marcos. They also led the government to force out such foreign investors as the giant U.S.-based grain trader Cargill and the Japan-based Mitsubishi Corporation. These were hardly the actions of a weak and dependent government, and they suggest that the Philippines may offer insight not just into the workings of a domestic political system but also into the role of the Philippines in the world economy. In this way the experience of the Philippines might have important implications for our understanding of other developing nations.

With these interests and concerns in mind, I chose to investigate Philippine politics and the role of the Philippines in the world economy. I looked at three separate sectors of the agricultural export economy: the coconut industry, the sugar industry, and the fruit products industry (primarily bananas and pineapples). I chose these sectors because of their importance to the political and economic system of the Philippines and because they illustrate both the nature of the Marcos regime and the ways in which the Philippines is integrated into the world economy. The coconut and sugar industries highlight the strengths and vulnerabilities of the Marcos regime, the ways in which agricultural export industries were used for political ends. The fruit products industry, in contrast, because it is so dominated by multinational corporations, both internationally and domestically, illustrates the limits beyond which even a strong state or a politically aggressive regime cannot stray.

My theoretical concerns extend beyond the substantive issues of the agricultural export industries, for those issues must be interpreted within the context of Philippine politics. The Marcos coup overthrew a working democracy; but it also overthrew the regnant paradigm of Philippine politics.

In the search for a new paradigm many observers have attempted to explain the nature of the Marcos regime, chiefly by close examination of the Marcos government's policies with respect to various sectors of the economy or segments of society. There have been excellent studies of labor relations, agrarian reform, government-media relations, government-church relations, and human and civil liberties in the country.[51] For the most part, however, these studies have focused on the impact of authoritarianism without developing a dynamic model of Philippine politics.

Another body of research has focused on the role of international actors in the declaration of martial law, the opening of the economy to foreign capital, and the development of a corps of Filipino technocrats which collaborates with external actors in the control of the Philippine economy.[52] Such works tend to focus almost exclusively on the power of the external actor, so much so in some cases that the political scene in the Philippines is portrayed as devoid of indigenous actors; the nation and its people become historical subjects with little hand in shaping their own destiny.[53]

What we need is a way of visualizing Philippine politics which captures the pressures that arise both from the international environment and from the domestic environment. The Philippines exists in a world market, where it occupies a particular place in the international division of labor. This place has in large part been determined by its history as an agricultural exporter and by the social and political structures that flourish in such an environment. The nation is also subject to pressure from the World Bank, from the International Monetary Fund, and from foreign investors. In addition, the country is enmeshed in a network of security agreements with the United States; it fulfills an important function in America's overall defense plans.

There are also domestic political pressures. The political system under Marcos was not just ruthlessly authoritarian; Marcos did not depend entirely on the exercise of sheer coercive power. In the early years of martial law his government enjoyed some measure of popular legitimacy (in later years sharply eroded). After 1972, despite the outward appearance of one-man rule, Marcos carefully constructed ruling coalitions, negotiated political compromises, implemented policies with a careful eye to their effect on important constituencies, and surrendered (albeit, rarely) to pressure, both domestic and international. But this is not to say that the focus of all studies of Philippine political economy should be the man at the center of domestic and international interaction. To focus on Marcos alone would certainly help us understand his regime and its policies, but it would also blind us to larger and, perhaps, more subtle patterns of change.

In his critique of O'Donnell's thesis that the end of ISI and the need for new models of economic development led to the assumption of power by bureaucratic-authoritarian regimes, Fernando Henrique Cardoso has argued that "the economic policies implemented in Venezuela, Mexico, Argentina, and Brazil are quite similar, but their political regimes are clearly distinct." He also points out that "what counts in [the choice of industrialization policies] is the character of the state rather than the regime. . . ."[54] Throughout the Third World an orthodoxy has emerged regarding the proper path to development (open economies, freedom for the international flow of capital, emphasis on increased exports, limited roles for governments). This orthodoxy has grown within an extraordinary diversity of regimes, lending credence to the argument of Cardoso—there are larger patterns of change at work in the Third World which must be examined at the level of the state.

Use of the state as a conceptual tool has, however, resulted in a great deal of confusion in the discipline of political science. Many authors use the terms state and government interchangeably. Others differentiate between a state and a government. Raymond Duvall and John Freeman believe that "the state is the public administrative apparatus as a coherent total. It is different from the government which is the set of persons who collectively occupy the highest positions of central decisional authority in the polity. The government is a decision unit, an actor. By contrast the state is the organized aggregate of relatively permanent institutions of governance." For others, the state is much more complex. O'Donnell points out that the state "is not merely a set of institutions. It also includes—fundamentally—the network of relations of political domination activated and supported by such institutions in a territorially defined society which supports and contributes to the

49

reproduction of a society's class organization." Likewise, Cardoso and Faletto argue that "the state expresses a situation of domination, reflects the interests of dominant classes, expresses their capacity to impose themselves on subordinate classes."[55]

With these last two formulations—by O'Donnell and by Cardoso and Faletto—it is possible to argue that states are forms of class domination and that this domination can be exercised through a variety of regimes or governments, some of them democratic, others more authoritarian. This is helpful because it forces us to look beyond the type of regime to identify what class or class segments are dominant in the nation. One of the central questions for the remainder of this book is precisely that: What class or class segments have been dominant in the Philippines since martial law was declared?

Important as this question is for the study of the Philippine political economy, however, it is also important not to fall into the habit of visualizing the state either as an instrument of one or more ruling classes (usually either a domestic or an international bourgeoisie) or as a neutral set of institutions that simply process and implement the wishes of pluralist interest groups.[56] As David Becker has written,

> recent advances in the theory of the capitalist state make it impossible to go on treating the latter as either a monolithic "state for itself" or a mere executive committee of a dominant class. Rather, the state is "relatively autonomous," in the sense of possessing some initiative vis-à-vis the particular (especially short-run) interests of any private institution, class, or class stratum, and at the same time is itself an arena of class conflict whose actions manifestly affect class interests and power.[57]

This relative autonomy of the state in the Philippines and elsewhere notwithstanding, my discussion of the evolution of the Philippine polity and economy in this chapter has highlighted several recurring themes. One central theme is that Philippine society has been dominated by an agrarian elite. International demand for Philippine agricultural raw materials, American tariff policy, and Spanish and American colonial administrative styles have produced a class society and a class structure dominated by an agrarian elite. The Philippine class structure has shaped the nation's path to development in ways that differ from those of Taiwan and South Korea, where the power of an entrenched agrarian elite was broken after World War II.

Yet this elite has not been in full control of the state, and we cannot view the state in economistic fashion as a tool of the Philippine agrarian elite. For most of the twentieth century state policies have been the product of collaboration among a variety of groups, primarily agricultural exporters in the Philippines, consumers of those exports in the United States, and American exporters of consumer goods to the Philippines. During its colonial administration the United States constructed a transnational state through careful collaboration with Philippine leaders who would adhere to a model of development based on agricultural exports and close ties with the United States. That transnational state survived the grant of formal independence to the Philippines. The Philippine Trade Act, parity rights for Americans, and the security ties that bound the two countries together limited the freedom of the Philippines to act autonomously. The country did not even control the exchange rate of its currency. Later, after the Philippines had gained a somewhat firmer control of its own economy through controls imposed during the 1950s (controls imposed with the permission of the U.S. president), its import-substitution policies proved a boon to American manufacturers willing to invest behind protective tariff walls. Import-substitution industrialization developed a new transnational coalition in support of government policies biased against agricultural exports and toward investment in manufacturing for the home market.

The policy stalemate that developed at the end of the 1960s threatened both the transnational coalition of class interests which makes up the state and Marcos himself, the leader of the political regime in power at the time. At the time he declared martial law, the president had two tasks that were of paramount importance. He had to defend his own continued rule, and he had to protect the continued domination of society by a transnational elite. In the early years of martial law the seeming omnipotence of Marcos made it appear that he was firmly in control of the Philippines and that his regime was free of both internal and external political pressure. Later, in the waning days of his rule, it became clear that Marcos was becoming more expendable day by day as his dogged

51

defense of his regime made it more difficult to defend transnational class domination in the Philippines.

In this version of Philippine politics, martial law marks the emergence of a new, transnational coalition of class interests based on export-oriented industrialization and a new emphasis on agricultural exports. Martial law made it possible to implement policies that no democratic regime could ever have implemented. The prohibition of strikes and forced reductions in wage levels, for example, could never have happened in the 1970s without martial law. Likewise, the opening of the economy by way of reductions in tariff levels, the elimination of government subsidies for consumer goods, and the provision of incentives for new foreign investment would have been far more difficult had the manufacturers of the import-substitution sector been free to participate in an open political system.[58]

In the abstract language of the theory of the capitalist state, therefore, it is true that the Philippine state has been "relatively autonomous." The state was able to take actions that were directly opposed to the interests of one class segment—import-substitution manufacturers—when it moved to open up the economy and to remove protection for domestic producers and subsidies for domestic consumers. But there are important differences in the degree of relative autonomy which a state may possess. In the Philippines, much as in Brazil or Mexico, the import-substituting segment of the bourgeoisie remains more powerful than in South Korea or Taiwan. Also, as subsequent chapters document, associates of Marcos used state power in the takeover of the sugar and coconut industries. Thus the autonomy of the state described here has to be understood in a theoretical sense and as it is expressed in the specific context of Philippine politics.

It is a relatively straightforward matter to acknowledge the growing power of the state in the latter part of the twentieth century. It is more difficult, however, to define what the state is and what it represents. The state, as I use the idea in this book, has several essential characteristics. The state is, as Becker says, "an arena of class conflict whose actions manifestly affect class interests and power." But it is not merely an arena for class conflict. More concretely, as Theda Skocpol has argued, the state is "a set of administrative, policing, and military organizations headed, and more or less well coordinated by, an executive authority. Any state first and fundamentally extracts resources from society and deploys these to create and support coercive and administrative organizations."[59] These coercive and administrative organizations are at once a focus for political struggle and a means of political and class domination.

In addition to being powerful and autonomous, the state in the Philippines has indeed been an arena for class conflict. The authoritarian rule of Marcos enforced an agreement on the proper model of development, but under Corazon Aquino the Philippines has once again returned to open, even divisive debate over development issues. This return to democracy and pluralism, laudable on many grounds, means that the Philippines is unlikely to achieve the kind of state autonomy that served to accelerate the pace of industrialization in the other Asian NICs.

Finally, no matter what model of development is chosen, the benefits of development have never been distributed equally in the Philippines. The state in the words of O'Donnell, "also includes— fundamentally—the network of relations of political domination. . . ."[60]

The state is thus a set of organizations both coercive and administrative, and these organizations have at different times in Philippine history provided an arena for class conflict. More often, though, the state has been an instrument for class domination. The relationship between state and various class segments determines the targets of class domination, and in some circumstances the state may even attack certain segments of the bourgeoisie. Standing above all these characteristics of the state, however, is one priority: that the state defend the general interests of capital.

It is important to keep in mind the key distinction between state and regime, for some actions taken by Marcos can be interpreted only in the context of domestic politics and his attempts to solidify his own regime. In this category are the actions he took against specific foreign investors in the agricultural export sector, his protection of and favoritism toward close friends (known in the Philippines as cronies), and his creation of export monopolies under the control of his close associates. Each of these actions by the Marcos regime was the subject of concerted, if belated and limited, opposition from the World Bank, the International Monetary Fund, and the U.S. government.

The case studies that follow are part of this interplay of two complementary and at times contradictory trends, the defense of the Marcos regime and the reconsolidation of class domination in the Philippines around a new, export-oriented model of development. What happened in the coconut, sugar, and fruit products industries is an integral part of both trends. Marcos certainly asserted tighter personal and national control over agricultural exports, and the story of how these industries were used to strengthen and legitimize Marcos's authoritarian rule is told in the next three chapters. But the actions of the Marcos government with respect to the agricultural export industries were also important for the reconsolidation of class domination in the Philippines around a new, export-oriented version of development. This second theme is more fully developed in Chapter 5, when discussion returns to the theme of regime and state and to the broader concerns of contemporary Philippine politics.

We now know that Marcos ultimately failed in both projects. He failed to defend his own regime, and he failed to reconsolidate class domination in support of export-oriented industrialization. His authoritarian rule had all the trappings—all the coercive and administrative machinery—of the bureaucratic-authoritarian industrializing regimes of Northeast Asia. Yet the Philippine class structure and the nature of its export economy make the country resemble not Northeast Asia but the NICs of Latin America—with a large agricultural export sector and a politically powerful ISI sector. The return to elite democracy in this uniquely Philippine context requires an explanation that incorporates both the personal and the structural levels of analysis.

CHAPTER TWO

The Coconut Industry

The coconut industry was the subject of a great deal of complex political maneuvering during the Marcos years. It was transformed from an industry with little government regulation to one dominated by a quasi-state monopoly over both the milling of the raw material and the export of oil and other coconut products. The monopoly was established by a series of presidential decrees and administered by close political associates of President Marcos— Eduardo Cojuangco, Jr., and Minister of Defense Juan Ponce Enrile.

This chapter sketches the history of the industry and its subsequent monopolization. The early history of the industry illustrates the strength of the agrarian elite. It also demonstrates how the nature of the political economy that developed during the colonial era shaped internal political and economic structures. More recent history indicates how the agricultural export industries have been primary beneficiaries of policies designed to shift incentives away from import substitution and toward export promotion. The bulk of this chapter, however, deals with the manipulation of the industry in ways that frustrated the goals of technocrats and consolidated the political control of President Marcos. We turn first to a discussion of the industry's importance.

Importance of the Industry

By most standards the coconut industry is, next to rice, the largest and most important in the Philippines. In 1978, of the 11,749,300 hectares planted to agricultural crops 24.6 percent, 2,889,800 hectares, were devoted to coconuts. Of the nation's $3.425 billion in exports 26.5 percent, $908 million, came from the export of coconut products.[1]

The Philippines is the world's largest producer and supplier of coconut products. In 1976 the country supplied 82 percent of world requirements. To produce this much for the world market, 86 percent of all coconut production that year went to exports; only 14 percent was consumed locally.[2]

Fully one-fourth and perhaps as much as one-third of the country's people depend for the bulk of their income, either directly or indirectly, on the coconut industry. Direct employment generated by the coconut industry in the late 1970s involved 450,000 landowners and caretakers, 50,000 owner-farmers, half a million tenants, and a million farmworkers.[3] These figures suggest that in production alone there are somewhere close to two million families, approximately twelve million people, dependent on the coconut industry. If we add in the many thousands of traders in the marketing chain, the workers in the oil mills and desiccating factories, and employees in management, the percentage of the population dependent on the coconut industry climbs even higher.

Structure of the Coconut Industry and the Nature of Production

There are now approximately three and a half million hectares devoted to the production of coconuts. The average coconut farm is approximately four hectares in size, which means several hundred thousand parcels of land planted to coconuts. Seemingly, each of these parcels has its own arrangements for ownership, sharing, and production. There are, however, some nationwide patterns that can be identified.

A general picture of the coconut industry comes from the Special Studies Division of the Ministry of Agriculture, which conducted a nationwide survey of the coconut industry during the years 1975–78.[4] This survey was comprehensive, and its findings remain pertinent a decade later. The survey included coconut farmers on 2,850 farms located in 248 towns and 32 cities in nine different regions. The producers were chosen at random from all sections of each area surveyed.

For the farms surveyed, the average cropped area was 4.87 hectares, of which 3.98 hectares were planted to coconuts. Average size can be misleading, though, because the 27 percent of the farms which were larger than five hectares made up about 65 percent of total coconut hectarage.[5]

Seventy-six percent of all farms were operated by the owner, 22 percent by tenants, 1 percent by part-owners, and less than 2 percent by leasees, caretakers, and others. Sharing arrangements range from 10–90 (with the lion's share going to the landlord) to 50–50, but the most common arrangement was 33–67, reported by 44 percent of share-tenants.

The men in the study were relatively old, averaging fifty-two years of age, and 41 percent of the men were fifty-six years old and above. The average size of household was 5.9 persons. The level of education for the men was quite low: 7 percent had no schooling, and another 56 percent had attended only grade school.

For all farms, sales averaged 185.62 pesos for nuts, 3,572.26 pesos for copra, and 55.29 pesos for fresh copra meat. Figuring in the noncash value of coconuts, total gross income averaged 4,462.38 pesos per farm, equal to 1,121.20 pesos per hectare. For all farms, the net profit averaged 660.11 pesos per farm or 165.86 pesos per hectare. At an exchange rate of seven pesos to the dollar, net profit was almost U.S. $23/hectare.

This income level seems exceedingly low, especially when we consider that an average of 5.9 family members must live on the net profit of 660 pesos or about $94. The amount of labor required to achieve this income, though, is also very low. The average farm, harvesting four times per year, required only 75.7 man-days per year or 19.4 man-days per hectare per year. In spite of this low labor requirement, the industry used a lot of hired labor, which, paid in cash, accounted for 65 percent of all labor used on the farms. Operator labor provided 20 percent, and family labor 13 percent.

The low income from coconut production and the small amount of operator or family labor invested in that production make it no surprise that most families had other sources of income. For all farms, and considering both men and women, the major source of gross cash income was the sale of coconuts and coconut products, which represented 48 percent of the total. Cash income was also earned from the sale of other crops and livestock, and from non-farm work. The sale of livestock (for men) averaged 3 percent of the total, while other sources (nonfarm work, including limited sales of livestock for women) accounted for 24 percent.

Copra is sold to barrio buyers, or town traders, or directly to exporters, depending on where the farm is situated. Most often copra passes through several hands between the farmer and the miller or exporter. Consequently marketing costs are high, and the farmers' share of the Manila price of copra is often as little as two-thirds. This problem is compounded by the fact that 45 percent of the 2,850 farmers reported they had received cash advances. This practice generally ties the farmer to the particular barrio buyer who has provided the cash advance, and the farmer cannot sell his copra elsewhere. Naturally, the practice weakens the bargaining power of the farmer.

A separate study found the distribution of profits in the coconut industry to be 24.6 percent to tenants, 44.6 percent to landowners, 4.6 percent to overseers, 12.3 percent to barrio buyers, 6.2 percent to town dealers, and 7.7 percent to exporters.[6] When the tenants' share of profits is low, tenants have little incentive for improving the cultivation of coconut. Yield per tree is low in the Philippines, and fertilizer use is also very low (2.9 kilos/hectare).

The advent of the Coconut Consumers Stabilization Fund Levy (to be discussed below) created another problem for farmers. The levy was supposed to be assessed on the first sale of copra. In return, the farmer was supposed to get a Coco Fund receipt that entitled the holder to certain privileges (for example, shares of stock in the United Coconut Planters Bank) and to membership in the Philippine Coconut Producers Federation (COCOFED).

Fifty-nine percent of the farmers received Coco Fund receipts, although only 45 percent took the necessary step of registering their receipts with COCOFED. Thus only 26.5 percent were eligible for the benefits that came with the receipts. The others lost their receipts, threw them away, or, what is probably most common, gave them to landlords.

It seems fair to suggest that the nation's millions of coconut producers lead a pretty bleak existence. These Filipinos are older than average, less well-educated, and have lower-than-average incomes. If coconuts give a coconut family an average net income of only 660 pesos, and this is 48 percent of total income, then total family income must be approximately 1,300 pesos per year—a per capita annual income of less than 250 pesos (under $36). The people most vulnerable to malnutrition, a 1978 survey found, were those with per capita incomes of less than 250 pesos and whose household heads were classified as farmworkers and small fishermen. Almost 52 percent of those who had per capita incomes below 250 pesos received less than four-fifths of the adequate energy intake.[7] Any expansion of the coconut industry is thus likely to expand the number of people living in poverty and malnutrition.

EARLY HISTORY OF THE INDUSTRY

The coconut is an indigenous tropical plant that probably has always served an important part of the subsistence needs of the Filipinos. The formal beginning of a coconut industry can be linked to a decree in 1642 by the Spanish governor, Hurtado de Corcuera, which ordered village chiefs to plant two hundred trees each and others one hundred trees. The decree was aimed at providing food for natives and soldiers and at producing caulking and rigging for the galleons.[8]

Exports during the Spanish era were dominated by sugar and abacá. The export of copra did not begin until the latter nineteenth century when the Western European and American manufacturers of soaps and margarine began turning to tropical oils as a source of raw materials.

The earliest available records of copra exports from the Philippines show that thirty-seven tons of Philippine copra valued at $1,940 were shipped in 1866 to Europe. It was not until 1900 that the first shipment of copra was made to the United States. By 1899 over 15,000 metric tons were being shipped overseas, and the quantities exported were rising rapidly. As a measure of growing demand, by 1910 there were already 208,000 hectares planted to coconut.[9] Exports of copra and coconut oil from 1899 to 1940 are shown in Appendix III.

In the years before World War I copra exports rose at a fairly rapid rate; the exports went to Europe and the United States. The first coconut oil mill was set up in 1906, and other pioneering coconut oil mills included Proctor and Gamble Manufacturing Corporation (PMC), a fully owned subsidiary of the American Proctor and Gamble Company, which started operations in 1914. The forerunner of the Philippine Refining Company (PRC) was begun in 1915. PRC was operated under the control of Lever Brothers Company of Cambridge, Massachusetts, part of the American branch of the British firm Unilever.[10]

The oil produced in these mills was primarily for domestic use until World War I stimulated coconut oil exports. The shortage of shipping provided an incentive to crush the bulky copra in the Philippines. Coconut oil, moreover, has a high glycerine content, which found a ready use in the production of explosives.

The war boom resulted in the construction of some thirty-seven coconut oil mills mostly in Manila. Coconut oil exports shot up from 5,000 tons in 1913 to 140,000 tons in 1919 with a record value of $37 million. The next year, however, with the war over, exports dropped to 77,000 tons and almost all the mills went out of business.

The only thing that saved the industry was the tariff protection it received in the U.S. market from the Emergency Act of 1921. The Act placed a duty of 2.67 cents per pound on coconut oil (subsequently reduced to 2 cents a pound by the Tariff Act of 1922). Previously there had been no duty on coconut oil. The Philippines did not have to pay the duty, of course, because of its status as a U.S. colony, and it thus received a tremendous advantage over other producers of coconut oil. Coconut oil exports began to climb again after 1921.

The temporary collapse of oil exports resulted in a shakeout in the industry, but by 1940 there were eighteen oil mills operating. Ten of these were small mills producing for the domestic market; the other eight were large mills producing primarily for the U.S. market.

U.S. legislation was also to have a significant impact on the Phil-

ippines in another part of the coconut industry. In 1922 the Ford-
ney-McCumber Tariff Act increased the duty on shredded coconut
meat from two to three and one-half cents per pound. This duty,
again, did not apply to the Philippines. The result of this tariff was
the establishment of the desiccated coconut industry in the Philippines. Before the 1920s almost all U.S. imports of desiccated coconut had come from Ceylon. By 1936 over a million dollars had
been invested in ten desiccated coconut mills, and exports during
the last half of the 1930s averaged about $4 million a year.

There is considerable evidence that the coconut industry in general, and coconut oil and desiccated coconut in particular, was the
direct beneficiary of the policy of free trade between the United
States and the Philippines. Of particular importance is the protection that Philippine coconut products received in the U.S. market,
which shielded the Philippine coconut industry (and its U.S. investors) from competition with other coconut producers.

In 1934 the U.S. Internal Revenue Act imposed a processing tax
on coconut oil, subjecting copra processed into oil in the United
States to a tax of two cents per pound. As Philippine copra was not
subject to this tax, the Act in effect gave Philippine production a
price advantage of two cents per pound over competitors. Between
1929 and 1934 U.S. imports of Philippine copra had averaged 315
million pounds per year, 60 percent of all copra imports. Between
1935 and 1940, after passage of the 1934 Internal Revenue Act,
Philippine copra exports to the United States averaged 458 million
pounds per year, 94 percent of all copra imports.[11]

This same processing tax applied to all Philippine coconut oil
imported into the United States in excess of 200,000 tons per year.
Before World War II, however, the imports never exceeded the
peak of 189,000 tons set in 1929, and so the processing tax was
never applied. The United States continued to import 90–95 percent of all of its coconut oil from the Philippines.

Clearly, U.S. tariff and commercial policy was the most important factor in stimulating the expansion of the Philippine coconut
industry. Policy makers at the time expected that free trade between the two countries would result in mutual economic benefit,
that the profits from the industry would lead to growth and development in the Philippines. What was not so clear was how these
tariff policies would shape the subsequent political economy of the

Philippines. The expansion of the industry took increasing portions of arable land, incorporated more and more people into the production of a crop dependent on the world market, and made it increasingly difficult to shift incentives away from agricultural exports.

Without early, protected access to the U.S. market the Philippines would not have been positioned to dominate the world market for coconut oil. The land would have been taken up in the production of other crops, perhaps crops for domestic consumption, and investments would not have been made in further oil mills for processing coconuts, freeing capital for investment in other areas.

None of this happened, though. The Philippines went on to concentrate on the production of an agricultural commodity for which prices fluctuated dramatically. It was a commodity, moreover, from which the Philippines gained little in terms of value added by downstream processing.

The Coconut Industry after Independence

World War II brought the closure or destruction of most of the nation's coconut oil mills and a break in the export of coconut products to the United States. The export of copra and desiccated coconut was rapidly restored after the fighting ended. Interestingly, though, it was not until the lifting of exchange controls in 1962 that coconut oil exports matched the level of exports achieved before World War II (compare Appendixes III and IV).

In the late 1950s the pioneers in the oil-milling industry (Philippine Refining Company and Proctor and Gamble) began to concentrate on further processing of coconut oil, mainly into soaps and detergents. This development almost certainly resulted from the import-substitution industrialization policies of the 1950s, because previously both companies had exported coconut oil and shipped finished products to the Philippines.

The other companies that concentrated on coconut oil exports did not benefit from ISI policies. In fact, they had to turn their foreign exchange earnings over to the Central Bank at the official exchange rate. This requirement, plus the 200,000-ton limit set on duty-free imports to the U.S. market, kept investments in the co-conut-oil-milling industry down during the 1950s.

In the 1960s, after the lifting of exchange controls, the incentives for investment changed, and as a consequence there was a big jump in the hectarage planted to coconuts. Several companies expanded their oil-milling capacity, and other companies decided to close down their U.S. operations and crush the bulky copra into oil in the Philippines. Pan Pacific Commodities of Los Angeles, which built the Legaspi Oil Mills, is one good example of this decision. By 1968, twenty-eight coconut oil mills were operational.

Part of the growth in Philippine coconut-oil-milling can also be traced to the fact that by the 1950s, imported coconut oil posed virtually no threat to U.S. farming and oil interests. The United States had become the world's largest exporter of oils, and import-ed coconut oil was only a small portion of the total oil used. In addition, there had been a large decline in the consumption of coconut oil for such food uses as margarine. Coconut oil was being used more in detergents and other industrial uses, where it com-peted with a wide range of nonedible oils such as petroleum derivatives.[12]

In the 1950s and 1960s the Philippines, from its secure base as the major U.S. supplier, went on to achieve world domination in the production of coconut oil. In 1970 it produced 66.3 percent of the world's coconut oil exports; this rose to 72.8 percent in 1975. But to say that the Philippines as a nation dominated the market for coconut products can be deceiving. The firms exporting co-conut products often were not owned by Filipinos, as Table 2.1 shows.

The 1960s and 1970s were a period of rapid expansion in the coconut industry. The lifting of controls in 1962, followed by two devaluations of the peso in 1962 and 1970, encouraged exports. To increase exports new investments had to be made in production. Investment in new plantings doubled the number of coconut trees between 1967 and 1978, as Table 2.2 shows. While Philippine pro-duction was rising, world demand for copra and coconut was also going up. In 1970 the world demand for copra and oil was 1.05 million metric tons; by the 1978–79 crop year demand had grown by 40 percent, to 1.42 million metric tons.[13]

The increase in copra production, coupled with rising world

63

Table 2.1. Major corporations in the Philippine coconut industry and the nationality of owners, 1965

Names of firms	Nationality	Percentage of total volume exported
Coconut Oil Mills		
1. Lu Do and Lu Ym Corp.	Chinese	44.0
2. Legaspi Oil Co., Inc.	American	24.8
3. Imperial Veg. Oil Co.	Chinese	9.1
4. Wee Kun Coprax Ind. Co., Inc.	Chinese	7.1
5. Phil. Refining Co., Inc.	English	4.9
6. San Pablo Oil Mfg. Co.	American[a]	4.5
7. Unifood Mfgrs., Inc.	Filipino	4.0
8. Batjak, Inc.	American	0.6
9. Proctor and Gamble (PMC)	American	0.5
10. Lucena Oil Factory	Chinese	0.4
Copra Meal and Cake Exporters		
1. Lu Do and Lu Ym Corp.	Chinese	33.8
2. Legaspi Oil Co., Inc.	American	16.6
3. Proctor and Gamble (PMC)	American	10.9
4. Philippine Refining Co., Inc.	English	10.2
5. Imperial Veg. Oil Co.	Chinese	6.6
Coconut Desiccators		
1. Franklin Baker Co. of the Phils.	American	30.4
2. Peter Paul (Phil.) Corp.	American	20.4
3. Blue Bar Coconut Products Co.	American	17.6
4. Red V Coconut Products		
Cebu	English	13.1
Lucena	English	11.6
5. Sun-Ripe Coconut Products	Chinese	6.9

[a]Hicks reports this is a Filipino-owned company, but Securities and Exchange Commission records show that of the original subscribers in 1965, Charles Hultberg, an American, owned 11,996 out of 12,000 outstanding shares. In 1976 PVO International, Inc., added 11,998,000 pesos of capital and took over the corporation.

SOURCE. George L. Hicks, *The Philippine Coconut Industry: Growth and Change, 1900–1965,* Center for Development Planning Field Report no. 17 (Washington, D.C.: National Planning Association, 1967), Tables 10, 11, and 12.

demand and the investment preference granted to coconut oil milling by government policy, both the Investment Priorities Plan and the Export Priorities Plan, led to a surge in investment in coconut oil mills. In 1968 there were twenty-eight oil mills operational with a daily crushing capacity of 5,154 metric tons. By 1977, fifty-one mills were operating, with a daily capacity of 9,022 metric tons. And by June 1979, sixty-two installed oil mills were capable of crushing 11,049 tons per day.[14] This boom in the crushing capacity of coconut oil mills can be seen in Table 2.3.

Table 2.2. Growth in coconut hectarage, 1967–78 (in thousand units)

Year	Area planted to coconuts (has.)	Bearing trees	Nonbearing trees	Total trees
1967	1,820	189,157	54,507	243,664
1968	1,801	185,960	66,471	252,431
1969	1,845	195,205	69,258	264,463
1970	1,884	215,151	57,284	272,435
1971	2,048	238,432	58,569	297,001
1972	2,126	268,679	56,818	325,497
1973	2,133	245,022	70,172	315,196
1974	2,206	262,441	72,042	334,483
1975	2,280	283,559	63,089	346,648
1976	2,521	297,806	51,329	349,134
1977	2,741	313,567	63,352	376,919
1978	3,317	325,155	158,018	483,173

SOURCE. United Coconut Association of the Philippines, *Coconut Statistics, 1979* (Manila, 1979).

The Board of Investments was offering incentives under the Investment Priorities Plan and the Export Priorities Plan for new investment in coconut oil mills. It was also trying to rationalize the placement of new mills geographically, so that most of the new capacity was placed in the central and southern Philippines, where supplies of copra were growing. Much of the new investment was made by Filipinos, but multinational corporations also made significant investments. In 1974 the Ayala Corporation (60 percent) and Mitsubishi (40 percent) bought out the Americans who had established Legaspi Oil. Granexport Corporation, a subsidiary of Cargill, established the Granexport Manufacturing Corporation in 1976 and put up a big new mill capable of crushing five hundred tons a day. The Fuji Oil Company and C. Itoh of Japan, together with their Filipino partners the Aboitiz group and San Miguel Corporation, established the Southern Islands Oil Mills; and the Lu Do family of Lu Do and Lu Ym Corporation in Cebu City invested with the Jardine Davies Corporation in Iligan Coconut Industries.

All of these new investments should have represented a positive development. Downstream processing of a Philippine product, after all, should have resulted in greater accumulation of profits for the country. There was to be more employment, more taxes paid; and the position of the Philippines as the premier producer of coconut products should have been enhanced.

Table 2.3. Estimated cumulative and projected coconut-oil-milling capacity, 1977–80

Year	Company	Effective rated yearly capacity (metric tons)	Approved by Board of Investments
1977	Estimated cumulative total	2,649,600	
1978	Iligan Coconut Industries Corp.	90,000	*
	Mindanao Coconut Oil Mill	37,500	*
	Bicol Oil Mill and Refinery	7,500	
	Coco Resources Corp.	7,500	
	Laguna Insular Commercial, Inc.	7,500	
	Subtotal, 1978	150,000	
	Cumulative total	2,799,600	
1979	Samarland Coconut Products	15,000	*
	Southern Leyte Oil Mills, Inc.	37,500	*
	Cebu Coconut Processing Corp.	37,500	*
	Surigao Coconut Development	75,000	*
	Sulu Argo-Industrial	37,500	*
	Subtotal 1979	202,500	
	Adjustment—mills started in 1978	60,000	
	Cumulative total	3,062,100	
1980	Eastern Davao Oil Mills, Inc.	75,000	*
	Noroil Oil Mills	37,500	*
	Olasahar Oil Mills	37,500	*
	Peoples Industrial Coco Development Corp.	37,500	*
	Muslim International Development	37,500	
	Sarranggani Bay Coco. Oil Corp.	30,000	*
	Subtotal 1980	255,000	
	Adjustment—mills started in 1979	127,500	
	Cumulative total	3,444,600	
1981	Adjustment—mills started in 1980	150,000	
	Cumulative total	3,594,600	

SOURCE. Private Development Corporation of the Philippines, The Coconut Oil Milling Industry (Manila, 1980), Appendix L, pp. 124–25.

The plan, unfortunately, had a fatal flaw. The rate of increase in milling capacity was 19 percent per annum between 1974 and 1978, but the average rate of increase in copra production was only 3 percent per annum.[15]

The Philippine Coconut Oil Producers Association, writing in 1979, explained the predicament:

the increase in copra supply has not kept pace with the increase in the crushing capacity of coconut oil mills. The growth of the coconut oil milling industry during the past six years has been phenomenal.

From 1973 to 1978, the combined rated crushing capacity of the coconut oil milling industry increased from 1,438,000 metric tons to 3,421,000 metric tons of copra annually. Copra production rose only to 2,306,000 metric tons in 1978 of which 379,776 metric tons were recorded as exported.

As a result of the copra shortage, the Philippine coconut oil mills operated well below their crushing capacities. On an industry-wide basis, they operated at 57 percent of their combined capacity. For a coconut oil milling business to remain profitable, its mill must operate at no less than 90 percent of its rated capacity.

As a consequence, several oil mills have been forced to suspend or cease operations with the accompanying lay-off of their labor force. . . .

While mills are closing down for lack of copra, more oil mills are slated to enter into the business. There are 16 new oil mills which are under construction or which have been approved by the BOI for construction activities. Their completion will up the industry's rated crushing capacity to 4,378,110 metric tons of copra annually.[16]

Clearly, the Board of Investments had made a serious error in projecting supplies of copra. The board knew, based on existing studies that in 1970, 24 percent of all coconut trees, excluding those in Bicol and the Eastern Visayas, were more than sixty years old—at which point productivity begins to decline.

Until 1974 coconut oil milling had been eligible for incentives under the various investment priority plans. In 1975, however, it was delisted from the eighth priority plan, because it was believed that adequate milling capacity existed for expected copra supplies. But coconut oil milling was relisted for the ninth and tenth IPPs after 1976, when new studies showed that the nation's copra supply in 1980 could support additional milling capacity.[17] Thus the National Economic and Development Authority (NEDA) Five-Year Development Plan for 1978–82 states that "coconut production in copra terms is expected to increase by 6.0 percent annually in the next five years, rising from 2.7 million metric tons in 1978 to 3.5 million metric tons in 1982."[18] This projection flew in the face of a historical growth trend of 3 percent or less per year. Worse, it was made at a time when the potential for expanding the hectarage planted to coconut was diminishing with the decrease in the amount of open land available.

Here is a case of faulty planning by technocrats in government.

They relied on overoptimistic projections of the supply of copra and were carried away by the desire to cash in on high prices for coconut products at the time of the boom in commodity prices in late 1973 and early 1974. The BOI offered tax and other incentives to encourage investment in coconut oil milling, and the response was overwhelming. When the supply of copra did not match the needs of the new mills, the mills reneged on their loan payments and closed down. How did the government and the industry respond?

To understand the response of government and industry to the crisis caused by overcapacity, we must go back at least as far as 1971.

THE TAKEOVER OF THE COCONUT INDUSTRY

In 1971 spokesmen for the coconut industry were successful in having passed into law Republic Act 6260, An Act Instituting a Coconut Investment Fund and Creating a Coconut Investment Company for the Administration Thereof. The Coconut Investment Company was to be capitalized at 100 million pesos, subscribed initially by the government on behalf of the coconut farmers and paid from the proceeds of a levy set at fifty-five centavos on the first domestic sale of every hundred kilos of copra. (One dollar then equaled seven pesos.)

A government agency, the Philippine Coconut Administration (Philcoa), was named as the collection agent and trustee of the fund. After the full 100 million pesos had been collected, the investment fund was to be transferred to the Coconut Investment Company, shares in which had been given to coconut farmers in exchange for their levy contributions.

Fifty centavos of the fifty-five-centavo levy was to be used to pay back the initial government subscription. This 100 million pesos was to be used to finance loans to coconut farmers, to invest in corporations engaged in industrial aspects of coconut products, to finance the establishment of coconut mills or other enterprises that would develop the industry, and to finance research and scholarships.

Two centavos were to be placed "at the disposition of the recognized national association of coconut producers with the largest number of membership as determined by the Philippine Coconut Administration for the maintenance and operation of its principal office which shall be responsible for continuing liaison with the different sectors of the industry, the government and its own mass base." It was subsequently determined that the organization with the most members was the Philippine Coconut Producers Federation. By its own description, COCOFED was originally founded by prominent planters from Quezon and Laguna. It remains to this day an organization, at least according to its critics, dominated by the large landlords of the industry.[19]

If we take 1973 as a representative year, 1,871,258 metric tons of copra were produced. At two centavos for every one hundred kilos, COCOFED received a total levy of 374,251 pesos to support its national office.

The remaining three centavos of the levy were to be used for the setting up and continued operation of the machinery for the collection and acknowledgment of payment; the organization of municipal and provincial conventions of coconut planters; the organization, supervision, and conduct of regional conventions and a national coconut congress; and the production and dissemination of information. Much of this money, in other words, went to organize the local chapters and conventions of the recognized national organization, COCOFED.

Republic Act 6260 provided the funding and national recognition that made COCOFED the unchallenged representative of the coconut industry. This was just the start of the important role that COCOFED came to play in the coconut industry. Also, and perhaps of equal importance, the Act established the precedent of using government power to collect levies and then turn the proceeds over to private organizations that claim to represent the interests of the entire industry.

Following the declaration of martial law, Presidential Decree No. 232 was issued, effective June 30, 1973. It established the Philippine Coconut Authority (PCA) and abolished the Coconut Coordinating Council, the Philippine Coconut Administration, and the Philippine Coconut Research Institute. The decree centralized the control of the coconut industry in the hands of a single agency.

It was at this time, in late 1973, that the commodity boom began.

With it came a tremendous jump in the world market price for coconut products. Naturally the domestic price for coconut products also rose rapidly. Table 2.4 shows the magnitude of these price increases.

On August 20, 1973, with the domestic price of cooking oil skyrocketing, PD No. 276 was issued. The decree gave the PCA the authority to place a levy of fifteen pesos on every hundred kilos of copra at initial sale in accordance with the mechanism set under Republic Act 6260, effectively raising the levy from fifty-five centavos to fifteen pesos for every hundred kilos of copra. The PCA was ordered to use the proceeds of this levy to implement a stabilization scheme for coconut-based consumer goods, which was the start of the Coconut Consumers Stabilization Fund (CCSF). The levy was to be temporary, lasting only one year, but the Philippine Consumers Stabilization Committee was set up and given the authority to revise the amount of levy imposed.

PD No. 414 followed, amending PD No. 232 by allowing, among other changes, CCSF to be used "to set aside funds for investment in processing plants, research and development, and extension services to the coconut industry." The decree was issued on April 18, 1974, and it is the first glimmer we get of the things to come for the coconut industry.

Table 2.4. Average monthly prices for coconut oil, 1973–75 (export prices are in U.S. dollars per metric ton, domestic prices are pesos per kilo)

	Export price			Domestic price		
	1973	1974	1975	1973	1974	1975
January	167.61	677.57	685.20	1.32	6.87	3.88
February	175.28	806.97	558.72	1.72	7.26	3.17
March	206.81	938.74	457.02	1.91	7.55	3.08
April	236.59	1137.55	418.50	2.21	7.41	2.94
May	243.52	1076.76	416.03	2.65	7.11	2.42
June	313.98	1087.50	348.94	2.83	7.50	2.15
July	373.14	1092.86	321.04	3.32	7.16	2.47
August	437.10	1078.65	317.42	3.65	6.72	2.58
September	479.97	951.11	340.99	3.45	5.37	2.45
October	490.28	874.04	329.78	3.67	5.56	2.23
November	574.91	770.73	327.92	4.24	4.95	2.09
December	624.82	662.60	305.16	5.73	4.49	2.17

SOURCE. United Coconut Association of the Philippines, *Coconut Statistics, 1979* (Manila, 1979), Tables 52 and 56.

PD No. 582 follows on November 14, 1974, creating the Coconut Industry Development Fund (CIDF), which is to be funded initially with one hundred million pesos out of the accumulated levies of the CCSF. Subsequently the CIDF is to receive twenty pesos from the levy applied to the first sale of every hundred kilos of copra sold. This levy is now permanent; it does not matter whether the Coconut Consumers Stabilization Fund is operative or not, the levy for the CIDF will still be collected. (The PCA in the interim had been given the power to revise the levy and by this time had raised it to sixty pesos per hundred kilos of copra.) The CIDF is to be used to finance the establishment, operation, and maintenance of a hybrid coconut seednut farm and to purchase the seednuts produced there for the PCA to distribute them for free to coconut farmers.

A consolidation of powers for COCOFED, or the big landlords and politicians tied to the coconut industry, comes on December 26, 1974, when PD No. 623 is issued. The governing board of the government agency charged with control of the coconut industry, the PCA, is reorganized. Previously the PCA had a governing board of eleven members, among them the chairman of the National Science Development Board, the undersecretary of agriculture and natural resources, the undersecretary of trade, the director of the Bureau of Plant Industry, and the director of the Bureau of Agricultural Extension. Now PD No. 623 reduces the governing board of the PCA by removing many of the government's representatives. The new board is to have seven members. The chairman and the president of the Philippine National Bank serve as ex officio members. Of the remaining five members, three are recommended by COCOFED, one is recommended by the United Coconut Association of the Philippines (UCAP), and one is recommended by the owner and operator of the hybrid seednut farm (Eduardo Cojuangco, Jr.).

Then in May 1975 the directors of COCOFED pass a resolution to the effect that ownership by coconut farmers of a commercial bank would provide a permanent solution to their perennial credit problems. President Marcos responds with PD No. 755 on July 29, 1975, directing the PCA (now dominated by COCOFED members, including Eduardo Cojuangco) to use collections from the Coconut Consumers Stabilization Fund to purchase a bank. The bank subsequently acquired was the financially ailing First United Bank,

71

owned by the Cojuangco family. It was eventually renamed the United Coconut Planters Bank (UCPB). All collections under the CCSF levy and 50 percent of all collections under the CIDF are to be deposited, interest-free, with the bank until bank and PCA jointly ascertain that the bank has sufficient equity capital to service fully the credit needs of coconut farmers.

A subsequent decree, No. 1468, of June 11, 1978, provided the funding and legal framework for the purchase of coconut oil mills by the United Coconut Planters Bank. Section 9 of the decree, states that

> notwithstanding any law to the contrary, the bank acquired for the benefit of the coconut farmers under PD No. 755 is hereby given full power and authority to make investments in the form of shares of stock in corporations organized for the purpose of engaging in the establishment and the operation of industries and commercial activities and other allied business undertakings relating to the coconut and other palm oils industry in all its aspects and the establishment of a research into the commercial and industrial uses of coconut and other oil industry. For that purpose, the Authority shall, from time to time, ascertain how much of the collections of the Coconut Consumers Stabilization Fund is not required to finance the replanting program and other purposes herein authorized and such ascertained surpluses shall be utilized by the bank for the investments herein authorized.

The PCA and COCOFED now have the legal and monetary basis to purchase coconut oil mills. But how will they convince owners to sell their mills? If a mill is profitable, the owner has no incentive to sell, and COCOFED does not want to be saddled with only those mills which lose money. An interesting solution to this dilemma was provided by PD No. 1468.

Coconut-oil-based consumer products were sold at subsidized prices set by the Price Control Council. The subsidy was paid directly to the oil millers from funds collected through the CCSF levy. Section 2(a) of PD 1468 stipulates that "when the coconut farmers, who in effect shoulder the burden of the levies herein imposed, shall have owned or controlled, under Section 9 and 10 herein, oil mills and/or refineries which manufacture coconut-based consumer products, only such oil mills and/or refineries shall be entitled to the subsidy herein authorized."

The funds from the CCSF levy and the CIDF were thus diverted to a new fund, known as the Coconut Industry Investment Fund (CIIF). Hereafter the subsidy to oil mills, designed to lower the price of consumer products, can go only to mills that had been purchased by the UCPB with funds from the Coconut Industry Investment Fund.

Business Day, reporting on a 1980 study by the United Coconut Association of the Philippines, found the proceeds of the CCSF levy (sixty pesos per hundred kilos) were being divided as follows:[20]

20 pesos for the Coconut Industry Development Fund (hybrid seed-nut farm)
12 pesos for subsidizing coconut-based consumer products
8 pesos for the Coconut Industry Investment Fund
15 pesos for mutual protection and assistance to farmers (scholarships, life insurance, etc.)
2 pesos for research
3 pesos for COCOFED.

By September 1, 1980, the Coconut Consumers Stabilization Fund had accumulated a total of 5.95 billion pesos, 5.7 billion of this total from the levy. Some 5.8 billion had been disbursed as follows:

subsidy payments for coconut-based processing firms, 1.5 billion pesos or 24.1 percent;
refunds to farmers amounted to 563 million pesos or 9.7 percent;
payment to the government for premium duties, 265 million pesos or 4.6 percent;
PCA operations, including research, fertilizer, and investment, 567 million pesos or 9.8 percent;
COCOFED grants and scholarships, 308 million pesos or 5.5 percent;
Coconut Industry Development Fund for the hybrid seednut farm, 2.2 billion pesos or 37.9 percent;
Coconut Industry Investment Fund, 389 million pesos;
22 million pesos for operational costs, refunds, short levy, and bank charges.[21]

73

The series of presidential decrees between 1973 and 1978 legitimized COCOFED as the sole representative of the coconut industry, reorganized the PCA under COCOFED control, provided the legal and monetary basis for COCOFED to purchase a bank and coconut oil mills, and withheld subsidy payments to oil mills not controlled by COCOFED. Following PD No. 1468 in mid-1978 a burst of activity reflected the changed conditions in the coconut industry. The changes unfolded like this:

June 1978—PD No. 1468 is issued authorizing the UCPB to purchase coconut oil mills and refineries on behalf of the coconut farmers.

October 16, 1978—The Board of Investments rules that it cannot issue tax-free certification to the UCPB for the importation of capital equipment for three proposed coconut oil mills and refineries. The grounds cited are adequate capacity of current oil mills plus the fact that refineries are not listed in the Investment Priorities Plan.

1978—Coconut oil millers reportedly lose an aggregate sum of $75 million on their operations.

January 1979—Legaspi Oil Mills, the nation's largest coconut oil mill, owned jointly by the Ayala Corporation and Mitsubishi, is sold to the United Coconut Planters Bank.

February 1979—Legaspi Oil Mills is paid for in cash, 158 million pesos, and UCPB takes over full management on February 15, 1979.

February 27, 1979—The Philippine Coconut Authority receives approval from the president for a memorandum to the National Economic and Development Authority which, in effect, lowers the premium export duties on copra by 62 percent and coconut oil by 48 percent. Coconut oil millers express concern that the new premium duties will encourage further exportation of copra and aggravate the shortage in the domestic market.

March 1979—The Philippine Coconut Oil Producers Association announces that the shortfall of copra supply has forced seven mills to cease operations. Mindanao coconut millers also seek the removal of the premium duty on the export of coconut oil.

April 1979—The Philippine Coconut Authority issues Rules and Regulations Implementing the Provision of PD 1468 That Only Oil Mills/Refineries Owned and/or Controlled by the Coconut Farmers through the Coconut Industry Investment Fund Shall Be Entitled to the Subsidy on Coconut-Based Consumer Products. At this time only three mills are entitled: Cagayan de Oro Oil Co., Southern Islands Coconut Oil Mills, and Legaspi Oil Mills.

June 1979—The Board of Investments recommends the complete abolition of premium duties on all coconut products and the increase of the export tax on copra to 12 percent, a move that would assist distressed oil mills. The PCA argues strenuously, both privately and through the newspapers, in favor of the status quo so as "not to make copra exports prohibitively costly in the world market."[22]

January–October 1979—The United Coconut Planters Bank takes over the ownership of the following coconut oil mills: Legaspi Oil Mills, Iligan Bay Mfg. Corp., Mindanao Coco Oil Mills, Iligan Coconut Oil Industries, Philagro Edible Oil, Inc., Cagayan de Oro Oil Mills, and Southern Islands Coconut Oil Mills.

September 3, 1979—Presidential Letter of Instruction No. 926 is issued. Section 2 states that "the bank acquired for the benefit of the coconut farmers pursuant to the provisions of PD 755 in its capacity as the investment arm of the coconut farmers through the Coconut Industry Investment Fund created by PD 1468, is hereby directed to invest, on behalf of the coconut farmers, such portion of the CIIF as may be necessary in a private corporation which shall serve as the instrument to pool and coordinate the resources of the coconut farmers and the oil millers in the buying, milling, and marketing of copra and its by-products. . . ." The Letter of Instruction also prohibits the licensing of new oil mills and gives the corporation it has authorized the priority to establish new mills should such mills be needed at a future date.

September 14, 1979—Five million pesos are transferred from Certified Account (CA) No. 506 of the CIIF for account to CA No. 001—1177-0 of United Coconut Oil Mills, Inc. (UNICOM) as per UCPB Board Resolution No. 147-79 as approved by the Board of Directors on August 29, 1979 in accordance with the PCA board resolution. Also on September 14, 1979, 495 million pesos are placed in a time certificate of deposit-private (No. 11958 of the UCPB) for five years for the account of UNICOM as per UCPB Board Resolution No. 147-79 as approved by the Board of Directors on August 29, 1979 in accordance with the PCA board resolution. Maturity date of the time deposit is September 13, 1984, and the interest rate on the 495 million is 12 percent per annum. Interestingly, the time sequence shows that the UCPB and the PCA approved the purchase of UNICOM on August 29,

1979. The Letter of Instruction authorizing this purchase is dated September 3, 1979. UNICOM was purchased from the associates of the law firm of Angara, Concepcion, Cruz, Regala and Abello on September 14, 1979. The Angara law office served as corporate lawyers to the UCPB, set up UNICOM in 1977, subsequently sold it to UCPB in 1979, and continued as corporate lawyers for both the bank and UNICOM.

First two weeks of November 1979—Granexport Corporation and Granexport Manufacturing Corporation, the two subsidiaries of Cargill in the Philippines, are sold to UNICOM.

February 8, 1980—More sales of oil mills are announced. It is reported that UNICOM now has thirteen oil mills representing 80 percent of the nation's oil-milling capacity.[23]

November 25, 1980—The text of PD No. 1644 is finally released, although it was signed much earlier, on October 4, 1979. This decree grants to the PCA the power to impose floor and ceiling prices in exports of all coconut products. The decree also appoints UNICOM as the sole corporation that can export coconut products to socialist countries.

Analysis of the Coconut Industry Takeover

By early 1980 the coconut-oil-milling industry had, for the most part, passed into the hands of the powers behind the United Coconut Planters Bank. Takeovers were concentrated in two categories, as can be seen from Appendix 2: foreign-owned oil mills, and newer, modern oil mills set up by Filipinos with incentives from the Board of Investments. The mills not taken over were generally the smaller, Chinese-owned mills producing small quantities of cooking oil for regional markets. These mills have, however, been deprived of any subsidy for the sale of their products, because they have not been defined as "farmer-owned." The other two exceptions are Philippine Refining Corporation and Proctor and Gamble, PMC. Both of these subsidiaries of multinational corporations are widely diversified down stream in the production of coconut-based consumer products. In all probability no takeover of these two was attempted because they would have been too hard for UNICOM to digest.

With the takeover of oil milling, one group captured the core of the coconut industry. This group controlled the export of almost all coconut oil and copra cake and also produced the majority of cooking oil for the domestic market. COCOFED also had ambitious plans to move into the trading of copra and to consolidate small coconut farmers into block farms, but these were long-range plans that would have been exceedingly difficult to implement. The desiccated coconut industry is still controlled by the multinationals, but it is of minor proportions compared to the milling industry.

Who was behind this transformation and takeover of the coconut industry? In the early stages the primary actors were the leaders of the Philippine Coconut Producers Federation. COCOFED leaders worked to get Republic Act 6260 passed, and they lobbied with the president in favor of an increase in the CCSF levy at a time when consumer prices for coconut products were rising rapidly. This lobbying they conducted in 1973, early in the martial law years, when emergency measures were being taken often without much advance planning. There was even some speculation that the military might take over the coconut industry.

With official government certification that COCOFED was to represent coconut producers, the federation began to receive a share of the Coco Funds. COCOFED now had the revenues to build up its provincial membership and to boost its lobbying efforts in Manila.

Leadership of the Philippine Coconut Producers Federation, 1980

Chairman of the Board	Rolando de la Cuesta
President	Ma. Clara Lobregat
Secretary	Domingo Espina
Treasurer	Eladio Chatto
Vice-President for Luzon	J. Reynaldo Morente
Vice-President for Visayas	Eusebio Moore
Vice-President for Mindanao	Anastacio Emaño
Directors	Magin Belarmino
	Jose Eleazar, Jr.
	Moises Escueta
	Jose Gomez
	Sulpicio Granada
	Bienvenido Marquez
	Jose Martinez, Jr.
	Iñaki Mendezona

In December 1974, when the Philippine Coconut Authority was reorganized, many independent government officials were removed from the board of directors. COCOFED control of the authority was solidified.

Board of Directors of the Philippine Coconut Authority, December 1974

Chairman of the Board	Rolando de la Cuesta
Directors	Eduardo Cojuangco, Jr.
	Ma. Clara Lobregat
	Hermenegildo Zayco
	Jose Eleazar, Jr.
	Governor Benjamin Romualdez

De la Cuesta, chairman of the board for COCOFED, is closely linked to Minister of Defense Enrile. He served as secretary to the Board of Directors at the Philippine National Bank while Enrile was chairman of the board there. Cojuangco is politically close to the president and owns the hybrid seednut farm on Bugsuk Island off Palawan. Lobregat is president of COCOFED. Zayco was the chief executive officer of Philippine Refining Company and later a governor for the Board of Investments. Eleazar is a director of COCOFED, and Romualdez, besides being the First Lady's brother, was a big coconut landlord in Leyte.

So the chairman and at least two of the board members at the Philippine Coconut Authority are members of COCOFED. Even members of the board who are not officially linked to COCOFED (Cojuangco, Zayco, Romualdez) can hardly be considered hostile to the COCOFED point of view.

When the PCA was given the right to purchase a bank for coconut farmers, it purchased the old Cojuangco family bank and set up a new management team.

United Coconut Planters Bank Management, 1980

Chairman	Minister Juan Ponce Enrile
President	Eduardo Cojuangco, Jr.
Director and Corporate Secretary	Jose Concepcion (Angara law office)
Directors	Ma. Clara Lobregat (COCOFED)

> Jose Eleazar, Jr. (COCOFED)
> Hermenegildo Zayco
> Emmanuel Almeda
> Narciso Pineda
> Rolando de la Cuesta
> (COCOFED)
> Danilo Ursua
> Iñaki Mendezona (COCOFED)

Executive Committee   Cojuangco, Lobregat, Concepsion, Ursua and Pineda

COCOFED again seems to dominate the management. The Executive Committee, however, is made up of three of the major stockholders before the COCOFED takeover of the bank (Cojuangco, Ursua, Pineda) and one member of the Angara law office. The investment arm of the Angara law firm, ACCRA Investments, was also a major shareholder in the bank before the COCOFED takeover.

Finally, in 1979 United Coconut Oil Mills was purchased from members of the Angara law firm and made the umbrella organization for control of the oil-milling industry.

United Coconut Oil Mills Management, 1979

Chairman of the Board	Minister Juan Ponce Enrile
President	Eduardo Cojuangco, Jr.
Directors	Jose Eleazar, Jr. (COCOFED)
	Iñaki Mendezona (COCOFED)
	Sigfredo Veloso
	Emmanuel Almeda
	Ma. Clara Lobregat (COCOFED)
	Douglas Lu Ym
	Jaime Gandiaga
	Jose Concepcion (Angara law office)
	Teodoro Regala (Angara law office)

This drama appears to have six major dramatis personae. Minister of Defense Juan Ponce Enrile is chairman of the board, UCPB and UNICOM; Eduardo Cojuangco, Jr., is president of UCPB and UNICOM; appears on the Board of Directors, PCA; and owns the hybrid coconut seednut farm at Bugsuk. Rolando de la Cuesta is chairman of the board at PCA, a board member at PCA, and on the Board of Directors, COCOFED and UCPB. Ma. Clara Lobregat is president of COCOFED, and a director of PCA, UCPB, and UNICOM. Jose Eleazar, Jr., appears on the Board of Directors of PCA, COCOFED, UCPB, and UNICOM. Finally, Iñaki Mendezona is a director of CO-COFED, UCPB, and UNICOM.

Also of special note is the law firm of Angara, Concepcion, Cruz, Regala and Abello. It set up UNICOM in 1977 before UNICOM was purchased by PCA. It continued to serve as corporate lawyer for the UCPB and UNICOM. It was a major investor in the UCPB, and its various members sat on the boards of directors of the UCPB and UNICOM. It is of some note that Edgardo Angara is also a member of the Sigma Rho fraternity at the University of the Philippines, along with Enrile and de la Cuesta. Enrile was once a senior partner in the Angara firm.

CONCLUSION

The history of the Philippine coconut industry under martial law appears to be a case of landlords using powerful friends of the First Family (Cojuangco, Enrile, and Romualdez) to gain a favored, government-protected position in the sector. The landlords have used the government's regulatory powers to raise billions of pesos, in the name of poor farmers and tenants of the coconut industry, and to turn the money over to their organization for its private use. They have also used the government's regulatory powers to put independent oil millers at a competitive disadvantage. As one millowner told me in 1981, he could see the handwriting on the wall. He went to Cojuangco to ask if he wanted to buy his oil mill. Though satisfied with the price he received, this owner claims he had no intention of selling out before the UCPB was formed and rules were implemented which granted subsidy funds only to what are called farmer-owned mills.[24]

Many of the millers who had made significant investments in the coconut-processing industry did so expecting that government interference in the industry would be limited to subsidies for exporters and, perhaps, to some regulation of supplies so that prices would not fluctuate too dramatically. These millers thought they had a friend and protector in the technocrat Vicente Paterno, a minister of industry and director of the Board of Investments.[25] They felt that the technocrats were in control of the economy and that, if necessary, Paterno would take their arguments to the president. The Board of Investments did argue for a ban on the export of copra, for the lowering of the levies on coconut oil, even for the importation of copra to keep the mills running; but none of these arguments was strong enough to sway the president's decision against the wishes of his political friends.

If the struggle in the coconut industry had been only a struggle between technocrats and politicians of the agrarian elite (represented by COCOFED), then it is likely that the technocrats would have been successful. They could have weakened the landlords and rationalized the milling industry, and at the same time they could probably have raised levels of exports and downstream processing. If we focus our analysis on the state, the technocrats were on the side of greater efficiency, a greater role for foreign investment, and greater export earnings. We would expect that the technocrats, along with foreign investors, the IMF and the World Bank, and the donor governments, would be strong enough to implement the new policies successfully.

But at the level of the regime another set of maneuvers was important. By 1981 the landlord politicians at COCOFED felt they were losing not to a group of technocrats but rather to the new management team at the United Coconut Planters Bank and the United Coconut Oil Mills; in other words, they were losing out to the political associates of the president.[26] While COCOFED was using the legitimate problems of oil millers and millions of coconut farmers to justify its own takeover of the coconut industry, it chose to work through close political associates of the president, such as Enrile and Cojuangco. To do so involved a calculated risk, for at the same time Enrile and Cojuangco were working to solidify their own position within the coconut industry and appropriating part of the surplus generated there. The articles of incorporation for both UNICOM and the UCPB stipulate that 5 percent of pretax profits should go to the Board of Directors and another 5 percent to the management team, including the president. No doubt millions, if not billions, of pesos from the coconut industry went into the Marcos political machine or left the country for foreign bank accounts. The technocrats lost and the landlords lost, because the coconut industry was politically important and because it was a source of surplus that could easily be tapped using the legal device of presidential decrees. At the level of the regime, therefore, the history of the coconut industry suggests that President Marcos wanted to accomplish two things. He wanted to weaken potential opponents from the countryside—the landlord politicians who had for generations dominated Philippine politics. Above and beyond this, he also wanted access to the funds generated by the industry.

The losers were the landlord politicians. Ultimately their defeat was to prove important, because in the countryside these were the people who provided leadership in the elite opposition movement that developed after the assassination of Senator Benigno Aquino in 1983. More important, the small farmers and tenants who were supposed to be the true owners of the UCPB and UNICOM were also losers. They have yet to receive any dividends from their alleged investments. Many of these farmers and tenants joined the opposition, either working and voting for Corazon Aquino during the 1986 election or, in numerous cases, offering their support to the underground New People's Army. Indeed, it was in the coconut-growing regions of the Philippines that the NPA achieved some of its most spectacular successes in the 1980s.

President Marcos broke up the old Philippine political economy where an agrarian elite dominated politics and society. This political economy had been shaped by colonial and neocolonial policy. Raw materials were produced by wealthy and powerful landowners and processed by an ethnically and nationally diverse group of investors; the processed products were destined for the world market. When Marcos took over, he weakened the landlords, drove out many of the foreign investors, and appropriated the surplus for himself and his machine. In doing so he alienated workers, tenants, and small farmers; landlords who were not incorporated into his machine; foreign investors who were not his joint-venture partners; and the nation's international creditors.

Marcos did not stimulate rational economic planning. The newly expanded coercive and administrative powers of the state were not used to generate economic dynamism and rationality. The surplus was not extracted for investment in new industry. Instead, the power of the state was used for individual political goals.

CHAPTER THREE

The Sugar Industry

Sugar is, from a long-term socioeconomic perspective, the most important industry in the Philippines. It was international demand for Philippine sugar which accelerated the incorporation of the Philippines into the world economy in the early nineteenth century. For decades, sugar has been the leading earner of foreign exchange for the country. And a disproportionate share of the nation's political and economic elite has come from its sugar-producing regions.

The Philippine sugar industry is, at its very core, based on great inequality. Its workers have never had the opportunity to reach their full human potential; recently they have had a difficult time even remaining alive. Yet until the depression of the 1980s in the world price of sugar, the industry also produced almost unimaginable wealth. Mansions, servants, luxury cars, and round-the-world trips were commonplace for the owners of the large haciendas and the sugar mills.

The surplus generated by the sugar industry, had it not gone into ostentation, might have been transferred out of the agricultural sector and into a program of industrialization. Many felt that was what was going to happen after President Marcos nationalized sugar trading in 1974. Prices at the time were exceptionally high, the surplus was controlled at the national level, and the potential for nationwide benefits was enormous. But instead, the industry today is in crisis—sugar planters are deeply in debt, many of the sugar mills are on the verge of being closed, workers are without work, without land to plant food on, almost without hope.

Sugar has since the late 1800s provided one-third to as much as one-half of the nation's export earnings. In recent years, as the economy has diversified and the world market price of sugar has periodically nosedived, the value of sugar as a percentage of total exports has declined (see Appendix 1). Export earnings, however, have generally exceeded $200 million dollars per year.

The sugar industry employed about half a million workers dur-ing the 1970s, 93 percent of them farmworkers. If we include dependents, the sugar industry supported around four million people, almost 9 percent of the country's total population.

The sugar industry is not important just because of the size of its export earnings or the number of senators and presidents it has produced. It is important also because of the social ills it has cre-ated. The status of sugar workers and their families has been a source of public controversy since at least the 1960s.[1] A now some-what dated but still illustrative study published by the government's National Wage Commission in 1977 found that the average sugar worker's family had six members.[2] These families, like all others in the low income brackets, spent about 60–65 percent of their in-come for food. The Wage Commission, in its attempt to determine the nutritional level of sugar workers' diets, compared the recom-mended daily allowance for Filipinos as prescribed by the Food and Nutrition Research Center with its own research on family income expenditure and the cost of nutritional requirements. Its findings show that in 1976, in the sugar-producing regions, a worker had to spend 19.28 pesos daily to purchase the nutritional requirements for an adequate diet for his family. The legally set daily minimum wages of the same year ranged from a low of 6 pesos per day for agricultural work to a high of 11 pesos per day for nonagricultural work.

The gap between required daily income and legal minimum daily wage is huge. Obviously the vast majority of sugar workers could not afford to eat a diet that met minimum recommended daily requirements. They certainly could not do so and also pur-chase other basic necessities of life.

These low income levels have a disastrous impact on quality of life, as a study commissioned by the Association of Major Religious

Superiors[3] graphically reports. Interviews were conducted on eighty-three haciendas in eleven milling districts in the province of Negros Occidental. Investigators found that workers had an average of only 9.07 months of work per year, 58 percent did not receive the minimum legal wage, and 80 percent of respondents did not get Social Security benefits.

Interviewers also asked questions that would illuminate the workers' standard of living. On the average each family had lost at least one child, 29 percent had lost two or more children, and 78 percent of children who died did so in the first three years of life. Ninety-five percent of the houses had no toilet facilities. In terms of common household utensils, the average family had five plates, four drinking glasses, two spoons, three pillows, two blankets, one mat, one fork, and one pot. There was one mosquito net for every two families. The study concludes its findings on diet with the observation that

> one who visits the families of sugar workers on the haciendas of Negros is shocked by the deplorable conditions of the housing but he is shocked even more by the visible signs of malnutrition especially among children. The bloated stomachs, the open sores, the listlessness, the lack of energy are themselves eloquent testimony of how cruel the system actually is.[4]

Conditions have worsened if that is imaginable, since the Association of Major Religious Superiors conducted its study. A report published in 1985 says that

> the situation in this supposedly once sweet "Sugarland" province of Negros Occidental continues to deteriorate steadily. An overwhelming majority of the estimated 400,000 displaced sugar plantation and mill workers throughout the province, their dependent family members, and the poor squatters of Bacolod and other cities and towns are suffering from severe malnutrition, starvation, disease, and lack of medical care, decent clothing and shelter.
>
> To understand the proportions of this inexcusable human tragedy, the province has a total population of approximately two million people. In an interview with this writer, Bacolod's Bishop Monsignor Antonio Fortich related that two-thirds of the children in the province and some 75,000 children in Bacolod alone suffer from 2nd and 3rd degree malnutrition.[5]

Under the administration of Ferdinand Marcos the industry did not prosper, nor did the nation prosper on the profits of the industry.

Up through the 1970s the Philippines had ranked tenth among the world's top sugar producers, contributing 3 percent of average world production or an average of 2.5 million metric tons per year. To produce this volume of sugar, about 450,000 hectares of land was devoted to sugarcane. Today, in contrast, predictions are that total production for the crop year 1986–87 will range from a low of 1.3 million metric tons to a high of 1.8 million metric tons.[6] Along with this decline in production under Marcos has come a corresponding increase in unemployment, starvation, and social tension. To understand these changes we must first look briefly at the history of the industry that Marcos took over.

THE SUGAR INDUSTRY IN THE TWENTIETH CENTURY

At the end of the nineteenth century most sugar was produced by individual farmers in wooden mills. Only the larger, richer farmers had been able to purchase iron mills. On Luzon Island, in the sugar areas closest to Manila, most of the farms were small and operated by tenants. In contrast, the large haciendas that developed primarily in less-populated Negros Island relied on wage laborers instead of tenants.

The nineteenth-century peak for exports was in 1895, when 376,000 short tons of sugar were exported. The Spanish-American War and then the Philippine-American War followed; by 1899 exports had dropped to 94,000 tons.

For the sugar industry, the first ten years of American occupation was a period of recovery from the setback it had suffered during the wars. To accelerate the rehabilitation of the industry, the U.S. Congress in 1902 reduced the duty on Philippine sugar by 25 percent. On August 5, 1909, Congress passed the Payne-Aldrich tariff law establishing free trade between the United States and the Philippines. The law, however, limited the amount of sugar coming into the United States free of duty to 300,000 long tons. This limitation was removed in 1913 by the enactment of the Underwood-Simmons tariff law.[7]

The establishment of free trade acted as both stimulus and guarantee. It brought U.S. money into the processing of sugar in the Philippines and thus sparked a technological revolution that reorganized the entire industry.

The first centrifugal sugar central, a major technological improvement over the old iron steam mills, was established in 1909 after passage of the Payne-Aldrich tariff, when Thomas Rous converted his old-style mill in Manaog, Pangasinan, into a centrifugal central. His was only the first of many centrifugal centrals set up by new investors from the U.S. mainland and Hawaii. (Appendixes V and VI contain a chronological listing of the building of sugar centrals.)

Sugar centrals were engineered and managed by foreigners, and initially most of the capital came from abroad as well. Millions of pesos were needed to build each central. Most of the big banks in Manila were owned by Americans, Spaniards, and Chinese, the number of Filipino banks was small, and the banks, in general, were cautious about lending for sugar ventures.[8] During the first half of the twentieth century, as a result, the sugar milling industry was, with few exceptions, dominated by foreign investors. Indeed, the domination of the milling industry by foreigners contributed to its early political strength. In combination with the local planter elite, foreign investors made a powerful political bloc that was able to control both the colonial state and the early postindependence state.

For some, however, such as the American governor general Francis B. Harrison, who were interested in the development of the Philippines and sympathetic to Filipino aspirations, the foreign domination of the sugar milling industry was alarming. Harrison's response was to recommend to the Philippine legislature the creation of the Philippine National Bank. The bank opened in 1916, its primary purpose to provide credit for agricultural producers, and the sugar industry soon became its number one customer. The bank was instrumental in the building of six new centrals owned by Filipinos, establishing a pattern of agricultural lending in which the bulk of credit is channeled to the politically powerful agricultural exporters.

Under the stimulus of free trade the Philippine sugar industry changed method of manufacture, from antiquated mills producing low-grade sugars called muscovados and panochas to modern factories producing centrifugal sugar. It took the industry twenty years to make the change, from 1910 to 1929. (The decline in production of muscovado and panocha sugars is given in Appendix VII.)

The rise of the centrifugal sugar centrals ended the independence of the sugar producer with his on-farm muscovado sugar mill. The planter was now dependent on the centrifugal central, which more often than not was controlled by nonplanters and non-Filipinos.

Sugar also became a pawn, and an important one, in the struggle for independence from the United States.[9] American sugar interests, having failed to eliminate Philippine competition through limits on landholdings or through tariff walls, began to push for Philippine independence—which would make the country's sugar subject to tariff duties. In practice, however, every independence bill after 1930 carried a provision that Philippine sugar be admitted on a quota, with that quota divided by allocation among Philippine producers upon the basis of recent performance. As a result, every Philippine central strove to increase its percentage of national output, and nearly every Philippine planter sought to increase his percentage of the central's output. Because of this quota race, total sugar production shot up while the independence question remained unresolved.[10] (For the effects on sugar production of the quota race, see Appendix VII and Appendix VIII.)

The end of the quota race came in 1934 with the passage of the Tydings-McDuffie Act, which set limits on duty-free imported sugar from the Philippines of 50,000 tons of refined sugar and 800,000 tons of unrefined sugar. Quantities in excess of these quotas were subject to full U.S. duties. Later in the year the Jones-Constigan Act adopted a sugar quota system under which *all* offshore supplying areas were given yearly annual marketing quotas to the United States.

The year 1935 marked the end of the boom for Philippine sugar. Exports to the United States dropped off by one-half at a point when Philippine sugar mills were locked into producing for the U.S. market. Production costs had risen behind the protection of U.S. tariff walls and were not internationally competitive. As a result of the limits imposed by the Jones-Constigan Act, Philippine producers had to reduce production. Limits and quotas were administered by the Philippine Sugar Administration (later the Sugar Quota Administration) under Commonwealth Act No. 4166, known as the Sugar Limitation Law.

Although these changes were certainly not the first example of government regulation of the sugar industry, they do highlight the dependence of the fortunes of the sugar industry on the actions of governments. It was the U.S. government that put an end to unlimited free trade and enforced a costly reduction in Philippine exports to the U.S. market. It was the Philippine government that then implemented the domestic limitation of sugar production and stepped in to regulate the relationship between planters and millers.

The remaining years before the outbreak of World War II were painful ones, in which the industry had to regulate its production of about 1.1 million tons per year, of which about 900,000 tons (100 percent of exports) went to the U.S. market. To achieve the necessary reduction in production, the hectarage planted to sugarcane dropped from 305,890 hectares in 1934 to only 166, 942 hectares in 1940.[11]

THE PHILIPPINE SUGAR INDUSTRY DURING AND AFTER WORLD WAR II

"The Philippine sugar industry suffered tremendously during the Japanese occupation from 1942 to 1944," according to Carlos Quirino. "Very little damage was done to mills and haciendas during late 1941 and early 1942 . . . the greater damage was suffered during the war years and at the time of the return of the American forces in 1944."[12] During the war years much of the sugar land was neglected or turned over to the production of food crops. Many mills, idled because of lack of sugarcane, were stripped by the Japanese to support their war effort or destroyed as the Americans reoccupied the Philippines.

Even if the industry had not been physically destroyed, there were serious questions about how it could survive without preferential access to the U.S. market. Hearings before the U.S. Congress in early 1946 concluded that,

as presently organized, it is obvious that the Philippine sugar industry, developed as it has been upon the American tariff protection,
cannot continue coming to the American market in competition with
U.S. sugar, unless it can be placed in the American market at the same
cost as Cuban sugar. Without an adequate period for adjustment, it
would be difficult, if not impossible, for the Philippine sugar to enter
the American or world market on an equal competitive basis with-
foreign sugars, except at the expense of present standards of living
and wages. Any reduction or impairment of these standards would
result in economic chaos and social disorders.[13]

This "adequate period of adjustment" was granted. The Bell
Trade Act of 1946 gave Philippine producers a basic sugar quota of
980,000 short tons to the U.S. market free of duty. This arrangement was extended by the Laurel-Langley Agreement of 1954 between the United States and the Philippines. The agreement maintained the same basic quota under a system of accelerating duties
based on a percentage of the full U.S. tariff. In addition, when war
damage payments were released during 1949–51, sugar centrals
received a total of 26.87 million pesos. The Philippine government
also formed the Rehabilitation Finance Corporation, capitalized at
300 million pesos, to assist in the rehabilitation of damaged industries.

But in spite of all this assistance, rehabilitation was slow. Short-
ages of work animals, implements, and planting stock, coupled
with the difficulty of getting the necessary parts for the centrals,
kept production low for most of the next decade.

A Philippine congressional resolution in 1952 prohibited the export of sugar to countries other than the United States. It exhibits
the strength of neocolonial ties at the time and reflects a realization
that in a world market dominated by quotas, loyalty to one's consumer is perhaps as important as having a ready surplus for
export.

The imposition of quotas on the importation of Philippine sugar
by the United States and the slowness of rehabilitation were only
two of the problems facing the sugar industry during the 1950s.
This was also the era of exchange and import controls. Some of the
families with extensive sugar interests were able to capitalize on
their land-based wealth to finance investment in the import-substituting industries or to diversify into banking.[14] Other exporters

concentrated on mobilizing their political power to oppose controls and, finally, to elect President Diosdado Macapagal in 1961. Macapagal had pledged to return to a free market economy.[15]

Such reactions in effect meant that the sugar industry was responding to its collective problems with a period of stagnation. (The evidence appears in Appendix IX.) From crop year 1951–52 to crop year 1960–61 the area devoted to sugarcane fluctuated around an average of about 190,000 hectares. Then in 1962 came devaluation of the peso. By 1965 exporters were no longer required to surrender even a percentage of their foreign exchange earnings to the Central Bank.

Also of great significance was the nationalization of Cuban sugar centrals in 1960. The United States responded to that nationalization by prohibiting the import of Cuban sugar in 1961 and raising the Philippine quota to 1.0 million tons (an increase of 300,000 tons over the quota set in the 1948 Sugar Act). The failure of various other countries to supply their quota to the U.S. market also increased the amount of sugar the Philippines could export to the U.S. market beyond its basic quota.

As a result of these changes in the U.S. market the policies of the 1940s and 1950s, based on the need to limit production, were reversed to support an expansion of the industry. Hectarage planted to sugarcane jumped from around 200,000 hectares at the start of the 1960s to well in excess of 300,000 hectares by the start of the 1970s. The increase in sugar production in the 1960s primarily resulted from the growing quota that the United States assigned to the Philippines.

This rising U.S. quota fit nicely with the political position of President Macapagal. He favored decontrol of the economy, and in this he was supported by the sugar exporters. In February 1962 he delivered a speech on the problems of the sugar industry in which he stated that he had acted "to provide economic leadership in the country by moving swiftly to restore free enterprise in order to enable all sectors of the economy, including sugar, to have a breathing spell in their operations and realize better returns from the fruits of their endeavors."[16] In line with this new policy, Macapagal approved the construction of two new sugar centrals.

After his election to the presidency in 1965 Ferdinand Marcos continued this policy of rapid growth. He challenged the industry to expand production by at least 300,000 tons per year. The machinery of government was also harnessed to provide support for the construction of new sugar centrals. Twelve new centrals started operations between 1965 and 1972 (see Appendix VI). And following the declaration of martial law in 1972, five more new centrals were constructed.

During the 1960s agricultural exporters were able to reassert their political and economic authority. Their earning power and political supremacy had been challenged and somewhat weakened by the import-substitution policies of the 1950s. Some members of this landed elite had also transferred part of their wealth into the commercial and industrial sectors of the economy. Yet agricultural exporters remained a potent bloc, one so powerful that (together with international investors and donors) it was able to get the policies that discriminated against agricultural exports overturned. Politically ascendant, they were in a position to respond dynamically to the growing Philippine quota in the U.S. market.

The experience of the Philippines differed in interesting ways from that of its neighbor to the northwest, Taiwan. In Taiwan the mainland Kuomintang political elite carried out an extensive land reform program after it moved to the island in 1949. Agriculture there was squeezed to feed the urban population, provide funds for industrialization, and earn foreign currency by selling products abroad. Members of the political elite were not landlords; they were separate from the small owners and tenants who benefited from the land reform program. Agriculture was clearly subordinated to the political and economic goals established by the state. And so the landlord class, having been weakened by state action early in the 1950s, was in no position to reassert its authority when Taiwan, just like the Philippines, reached the end of the "easy phase" of import substitution in the late 1950s and early 1960s. Stringent state control, the limited role of foreign investors, the narrow and restricted political sphere, and the absence of a landed elite, all made Taiwan radically different from the Philippines. The 1960s thus brought to Taiwan an increasing incorporation of its economy into the world economy as a low-wage exporter of manufactured goods. The island made the transition without significant political challenge or increased levels of social tension. In the Philippines, by contrast, the 1960s were a decade of industrial stagnation and reincorporation of the country into the world market as an exporter of agricultural goods.[17]

CHANGES IN THE SUGAR INDUSTRY IN THE 1970S

Before the 1960s sugar milling had been dominated by the "old elite," traditionally wealthy Filipino families along with a few remaining Spanish and American interests. Among the prominent families in the sugar business were the Cojuangcos (including the current president, Corazon Cojuangco Aquino), the Yulos, Lopezes, Aranetas, Elizaldes, and the Revillas. The development of new centrals, each of which required numerous government approvals and loan guarantees and cost anywhere from five to forty million dollars, was a project with almost unlimited prospects for political empire building. Each new central tied the investors to government sponsors, and it also diluted the power of the old elite, which had controlled the twenty-five or so centrals around which the industry revolved.

Most of the new centrals built in the 1960s were located in areas already dominated by sugar. In the 1970s, however, the sugar industry diversified to new areas, including Camarines Sur in Bicol; Davao, North Cotabato, and Bukidnon in Mindanao; and Zambales and Cagayan in Luzon. The effect was a further dissolution of the political and economic power of the old elite of sugar families.

All of this expansion was predicated on the beliefs that the Philippines would be able to ship ever larger amounts of sugar to the U.S. market and that it would also gradually diversify its markets. Nineteen seventy-five ended both beliefs. Sugar exports dropped to 972,217 metric tons from the previous year's 1,542,081 metric tons, largely because U.S. imports dropped from 1,275,699 tons in 1974 to 328,674 tons in 1975.

Two things had happened in 1974. The U.S. Congress had refused to extend the 1948 Sugar Act, which set quotas for imports from favored countries. It had done so in response to a world shortage in 1974 which had driven prices to a record high of 65 U.S. cents per pound. Also the Laurel-Langley Agreement had expired, and so Philippine producers had to pay full duties on all sugar exported to the United States. The Laurel-Langley Agreement and the U.S. Sugar Act had together provided protection and a tremendous subsidy to the Philippine sugar industry; indeed, for one year (1967) alone, the U.S. comptroller general estimated that this hidden assistance amounted to $97.2 million.[18] This assistance went not to the Philippine government but primarily to the planters and millers, and it was a major source of their political and economic power.

After 1975, for the first time, the Philippine sugar industry was exposed to the vagaries of the world market. Unfortunately for the country and its producers, the years 1975–78 were marked by a depressed world market for sugar, as Table 3.1 shows.

The low market price for sugar from 1975 onward, coupled with the end of preferential access to the protected U.S. market, spelled hardship for the industry as a whole and disaster for owners of new mills who had borrowed heavily to cover construction and start-up costs. Many of these loans were either from or guaranteed by the Philippine National Bank or the Development Bank of the Philippines. For mills where there has been trouble about repaying debts, the banks have installed their own comptrollers. In more serious cases they have taken over the centrals by turning their loans into equity. These troubled sugar mills were also severely hurt by the government's takeover of sugar trading.

In June 1974 a presidential decree was issued, a decree every bit as important as the abolition of Congress two years earlier in Presi-

Table 3.1. World price for sugar, 1970–1979 (in U.S. cents per pound)

Year	Average annual price	Percentage change
1970	3.69	
1971	4.52	22.5
1972	7.43	64.4
1973	9.61	29.3
1974	30.00	212.2
1975	20.51	(31.6)
1976	11.59	(43.5)
1977	8.11	(30.0)
1978	7.81	(3.6)
1979	9.66	23.5

SOURCE. Private Development Corporation of the Philippines, *The Sugar Industry* (Manila, 1980), 2.

dent Marcos's continuing effort to reshape the Philippine political economy. The 1974 decree gave the Philippine Exchange Company, or Philex, a subsidiary of the Philippine National Bank, complete monopoly control as the nation's sole exporter of sugar. It came at a time when world sugar prices were at their highest level ever, but Philippine millers and planters were not able to take advantage of this windfall. Their access to the international market was cut, leaving them dependent on the state and without the economic resources that had made them the nation's most powerful political bloc. In October 1974 Philex was buying sugar at 134 pesos per picul and selling to the United States at 470 pesos per picul, a clear profit of about 30 U.S. cents per pound.[19]

The takeover created two results, both of which must have pleased President Marcos. It provided a new source of revenue, and it took power away from any potential challengers he might face from within the sugar industry. The president's position was further consolidated when control of trading in sugar was removed from the Philippine National Bank and transferred to a new agency, the Philippine Sugar Commission (Philsucom), under the leadership of his close friend Roberto S. Benedicto. Philsucom had been established in 1974 by Presidential Decree No. 388 but was only activated in 1977 with the appointment of Benedicto, an old fraternity brother from the president's law school days at the University of the Philippines. Benedicto was also a regional director and treasurer for the president's Kilusang Bagong Lipunan (KBL), the New Society Movement political party, and had been ambassador to Tokyo in the late 1960s and early 1970s, when many of the new sugar centrals were being built by or imported from such Japanese companies as Marubeni, Toyo-Menka Kaisha, and Mitsubishi.

Under Benedicto the Philippine Sugar Commission and its trading arm, the National Sugar Trading Corporation (Nasutra), had not only sole authority to trade sugar, domestically and internationally, but also the power to set the price at which it purchased raw sugar from planters and millers and to set the price it paid millers for the milling of sugar. With these powers Philsucom was able to establish a distribution of income amongst the various sectors of the industry. In 1980, sugar planters felt that perhaps as many as 95 percent of their members had past due or restructured loans with the banks; only about 50 percent made a profit during crop year 1980–81.[20] By 1986 fully twenty-two of the forty-one sugar centrals had lost so much money that they were, in effect, controlled by the Philippine National Bank. At least eight were to be mothballed under the plans of the new Aquino government.[21]

While other parts of the sugar industry were struggling because of low sugar prices, however, Philsucom was apparently a center of capital accumulation. The Philippine government through Philsucom purchased three sugar refineries that were constructed on a turnkey basis by foreign contractors.[22] By 1980 Philsucom had also purchased eight of a planned seventy-six mechanical harvesters, each of which cost 1.4 million pesos (approximately U.S. $200,000 each at the 1980 exchange rate).[23] These documented cases of Philsucom investment are supplemented by widespread anecdotes. People in the sugar industry tell of Philsucom purchases of dredgers, warehouses, railroads, shipping lines, and large-scale infusions of capital into the Republic Planters Bank (whose chairman was Roberto S. Benedicto). Philsucom seems to have been the only entity in the entire industry to prosper and to make any new investment since the government used presidential decrees to create a monopoly in sugar trading.

THE NEW POLITICAL ECONOMY OF SUGAR

Changes in the sugar industry had a singular impact on the political economy of the Philippines. They were of primary importance in three areas: the cohesiveness of the political elite, the political strength of the Marcos regime, and the rise of social tension in the sugar-producing regions.

First, the sugar industry experienced rapid growth in the 1960s— an increase of one hundred thousand hectares in the area planted to sugar and a rise in the number of centrals from about twenty-five to forty-two. This, coupled with a diversification of the regional location of the industry, broke up the tightly knit old elite.

There may have been continual infighting over politics, and disputes between planters and millers over control of the industry were commonplace, but the unity and strength of the old elite of established, often mestizo, families went largely unchallenged.

Sugar interests not only produced the nation's most lucrative export, they had also come to dominate the banking industry. Scions of the sugar families were prominent in all sectors of the postwar economy, just as they were prominent in the social circles of the elite.

Ferdinand Marcos had as his vice-president before martial law Fernando Lopez, a member of what was then regarded as the wealthiest of the wealthy sugar families. After martial law Vice-President Lopez was discarded along with the Congress and the old Constitution. Among those able to threaten the continued rule of Marcos, the Lopez family was singled out for special treatment— the government seized their media empire, their power-generating plants, and other economic assets; Eugenio Lopez, Jr., was arrested and charged with plotting to assassinate Marcos; and the former vice-president was harassed even while in exile in the United States.

By 1974, then, the sugar bloc was no longer made up of a small group of interrelated and geographically close-knit families, and it faced the frightening example of what had happened to the Lopez family. The bloc did not mount any kind of effective opposition to the government's takeover of sugar trading. Sugar families had no access to the media, which were all in the hands of Marcos supporters. They had no access to a political forum, because Congress had been closed. They had no mass political base; they could mobilize their followers for elections but could not find the will to mobilize the population in challenge to a sitting president with martial law powers. Demonstrations and all political gatherings had been outlawed, and the only response left to them was economic.

Throughout the industry the people I talked with in 1980 repeated the same argument: they could not risk new investments or even maximize production in an environment of economic insecurity. Both Edgardo Yap of the Philippine Sugar Association and A. Gordon Westly, formerly of Jardine Davies (a major foreign investor in sugar), attributed the sharp drop in sugar production in the late 1970s to the variability and uncertainty of government action.[24] Planters such as Juan Yulo of Negros agreed at the time that many areas formerly planted to sugarcane had been abandoned and would not be replanted because planters had lost confidence in the government's marketing system.[25]

This unwillingness to invest in the industry was related to the second major change in the political economy, the strength of the Marcos regime. One member of a large sugar-planting family explained that Marcos was able to break the power of the premartial law sugar bloc because families in the bloc had such a large stake in the system. Their investment was so large, the problems of converting to other crops so difficult, and their debt so great that they were hooked into the sugar economy with no way to get out.[26]

An official of Jardine Davies likewise felt that if his company were planning any new investments in the sugar industry, the high capital costs and the uncertainty regarding administrative regulation made it important to have the government as a partner. The partnership would, he felt, insure fair treatment and a steady supply of raw materials.[27]

Neither domestic nor foreign investors invested new money in sugar during the martial law years. Their decision reflects not just the world price for sugar but, more important, the political uncertainties of doing business under the Marcos regime. The regime could not in the final analysis convince people that its rule was worthy of endorsement by new investment. It had the power to punish, to coerce, to squeeze the wealth from an industry, but it had no positive vision of the future. And what happened in the economic sphere was duplicated in the political sphere. In Negros and other sugar-producing regions Marcos chose to rule through the elite. Members of the elite willing to work with him survived and even prospered despite the general recession in the industry, and those who prospered because of their political connections always had the economic means to maintain their own local coalition of supporters.

There was, however, no organized political party. The New Society Movement, the closest thing the country had to a political party, was activated only for elections and then primarily as a vehicle for the political ambitions of the elite and Marcos himself. The strength of the regime lay, therefore, in its ability to extract a passive submission from the majority of the people to the will of Marcos. The president achieved this acquiescence through a variety of mechanisms. One was almost complete control of information: public knowledge about sugar trading was kept as limited as possible. Limited information made it easier for the government to argue that it was making the best of a difficult situation and that if sugar producers did have anything to complain about, it was the low price of sugar in the international market, not government manipulation of prices and extraction of surplus.

Second, in the primary sugar-producing regions there was an active campaign to built a reputation for Marcos and Benedicto as saviors and protectors of the industry. Roberto Benedicto was virtually omnipresent in the heyday of his leadership of the sugar industry. If there was a beauty pageant, he was there to donate five thousand pesos for the cost of the celebration. If there was a flood, he was there with fifty thousand pesos as disaster relief. In every case this was done in the name of the generous and enlightened leadership of the Marcos administration. And for those who could not be attracted to cooperate with the Marcos regime, there was always the example of what had happened to the Lopez family— the richest sugar family of all.

At one point in the early 1980s the Philippine Sugar Association (whose members come primarily from families that own sugar centrals) took out full-page advertisements in the Manila daily newspapers praising the government's actions. The text said, in part, "we feel considerable credit is due to the Philippine Sugar Commission and the National Sugar Trading Corporation in their exemplary and successful handling of many difficult situations faced since their inception and we congratulate you for your leadership and your efforts in keeping the industry viable, thereby maintaining its vital position in the national economy."[28]

The National Sugar Trade Union, sanctioned by the Ministry of Labor under Marcos as interlocutor for all sugar workers, was even more extravagant in its praise. The union's full-page advertisement, written in the form of a prayer to "Almight God Our Father," says among other things that "we, the workers in the sugar industry and our families, do raise our voices in thanksgiving for all the guidance you have given to President Marcos, Minister Ople, and Ambassador Benedicto that through their efficient and effective management of the sugar industry in crisis, most of us workers were kept on our jobs—and now we are blessed with additional fringe benefits."[29]

Workers who refused to accept the leadership of the regime's National Sugar Trade Union faced repression, and this is a factor in the last major change in the political economy of sugar I want to discuss—the rise of social tension and conflict. Before millions of middle-class opponents, shocked by the 1983 assassination of Benigno Aquino, Jr., took to the streets in the final struggle to oust Marcos, the workers of the sugar industry had been risking their lives in opposition, partly out of desperation, partly in the hope that something could be done to change the sugar industry.

In March 1978, for example, long before the Manila middle class was aroused from its quiescence, there was a peaceful demonstration in Bacolod City by 5,500 workers, students, and professionals to protest military terrorism. In December of that year 20,000 people attended rallies and marches throughout Negros Occidental. The theme of these actions was "Uphold Democratic Rights."

The churches and independent unions in the sugar industry did their best to organize workers and, with their limited resources, to document the many cases of murder, torture, union harassment, lockouts, and strike breaking that took place every day in the sugar-producing regions. The sugar industry is based on the inequality of class privilege and thus is also based on structural, if not overt, violence against workers. The evidence suggests that the Philippines experienced a rising tide of violence targeted mostly against innocent people whose only offense was to work for justice and a decent standard of living.

Caught between military repression and low wages, many workers got desperate. They turned for leadership to the churches, the National Federation of Sugar Workers, and in some places to the New People's Army. The level of consciousness among the workers is rising but quite varied. In the early 1980s, for example, workers I spoke with on Hacienda San Antonio near Victorias town, a typical hacienda, said that they were being paid 11.75 pesos a day (at that time seven pesos equaled one U.S. dollar) but felt lucky if they got two hundred days of work a year. They lived in bleak surroundings with few belongings and a meager diet. What changes would it take, I asked them, to improve their life, to make them happy? Many said they needed more pay, anything from 16 to 33 pesos per day. Those who had been organized by independent unions gave a slightly different response: they felt maybe 50 pesos per day would be fair, because that would give them a chance to educate their children so they could escape the life of the sugarcane worker. Union leaders had a longer-term goal—they were trying to organize workers "not just for pay increases, but ultimately for liberation." The union leaders and some of the workers recognized that control of the land was at the root of the problem and hence defined justice as more than simple wage increases.

Men like these workers are among the hundreds who have joined the New People's Army in Negros Occidental, making the province a hotbed of insurgency. Men like these workers also voted for Corazon Aquino for president and then risked their lives to make sure their votes were counted. Neither political tradition nor bribery could keep them committed to the continued rule of Marcos and his elite supporters. Nor did military repression work for Marcos; it only drove workers into the camp of the New People's Army.

Marcos succeeded in capturing the surplus of the sugar industry during the martial law period. In doing so he also destroyed the old political economy of the industry; new investment disappeared, old patterns of elite control broke down, and new patterns of political participation emerged. In the long run, capturing economic control of the industry was costly for Marcos. The president failed to introduce effective programs for national development of the industry and to ameliorate the inequalities that the industry generates. As a consequence he was challenged by a rising insurgency, and eventually, in what must have been a particularly bitter humiliation, he lost the presidency to the daughter of one of the nation's richest sugar-producing families.

CHAPTER FOUR

The Fruit Products Industry

Fruit products, unlike sugar and coconuts, are almost completely dominated by agribusiness multinational corporations. The three most important multinationals are Del Monte Corporation, United Fruit Company, and Castle and Cooke.

The domination of the industry by foreign-based corporations has had a definite impact on the evolution of the Philippine political economy. Plantation agribusiness, producing commodities that depend on extensive marketing and distribution chains controlled by multinationals, can succeed only in a particular kind of economic environment. The MNCs require that capital flow freely in and out of the country. They require access to extensive areas of land which are relatively contiguous. Plantations and canneries need dependable and relatively inexpensive labor. One consequence of these requirements is that investments have generally gone to nations controlled by governments congenial to foreign investment and closely allied with the West. The Philippines has met every one of these requirements. Each Philippine government, both before and after independence, as well as every Philippine president, has welcomed foreign investment in plantation agriculture.

Coconuts and sugar are sold internationally through established commodity markets that do not rely on brand consciousness or advertising. For the international marketing of these two commodities, it makes little difference whether the product is initially sold by a multinational corporation or by a quasi-state monopoly. The fruit products industry is vastly different.

The domestic processing of coconut and sugar products involves only limited foreign investment, which could be subordinated to the private political interests of Ferdinand Marcos with little fear of reprisal. The same does not hold true for fruit products. The entrenched power of the foreign investors in fruit products has limited the freedom of the state to manipulate the economy, and these are limits that even an aggressive political leader such as Marcos could not violate. Attempts to take over the industry would have foundered on the continued MNC control of distribution and advertising and on the ability of the multinational corporations simply to withdraw their investments. Conceivably Marcos or his political associates might have tried to use state power to buy out foreign investors, but any such attempt would have raised significant new questions about the investment climate in the Philippines, which, in turn, would have had a detrimental impact on Philippine relations with its international creditors and its ally the United States. Hence, one purpose of this chapter is to demonstrate the difference between agroexport industries that are dominated by foreign investors and those which are subject to predominantly local control.

As important as the multinationals have been in the fruit products industries, Marcos did strengthen his local allies in the banana industry and he did seek to enlarge the role of state institutions involved in plantation agribusiness. In these endeavors he enjoyed less success than he did in the coconut and sugar industries. This chapter thus illustrates in concrete ways how the power of both the state and the Marcos regime was limited. The foreign investor, at least in the case of fruit products, was too powerful a member of the "pact of domination" which makes up the Philippine state to be directly attacked by Marcos. In this sense it is clear that some segments of the bourgeoisie are more powerful than others. This chapter illustrates some of the factors that help determine the strength of the multinational agribusiness segment of the bourgeoisie.

In addition, the story of the fruit products industry highlights the ongoing nature of the incorporation of the Philippines into the world market, a process that extends far beyond the actions of the colonial and the early postcolonial state. During his fourteen years of authoritarian rule President Marcos sought to increase agricultural exports. In support of this goal he encouraged foreign investment in rubber, coffee, cacao, and African palm oil, as well as the more traditional export crops of bananas and pineapples. Now, after the fall of Marcos, Corazon Aquino's government has announced that one of its foremost goals in the economic development of the nation will be to increase agricultural exports and that this will entail new foreign investment. How Marcos dealt with industries where he could not establish his own firm political control is by virtue of his failure to dominate likely to be instructive as over time the Aquino government—a government committed to eliminating the political manipulation of industry for private gain—attempts in its turn to increase agricultural exports.

Foreign investment in Philippine fruit products forms three distinct periods. In the first the Philippines was still a U.S. colony. The second came after the reopening of the economy in the 1960s, following the period of import-substitution industrialization. As we have already seen, those years have been crucial in determining the subsequent path to development. Finally, there is the period since the late 1970s in which the Philippines has opened wide its doors to attract new investment in agriculture. This stage in Philippine development has not yet ended.

HISTORICAL BACKGROUND

Within the general pattern of MNC-dominated agribusiness in the Philippines, it is important to distinguish several important variations. These variations are linked in part to the time when the investment was made and in part to the system of land acquisition and control.

The earliest multinational investment in the Philippines for the production and export of fruit products was made in 1928, when the California Packing Corporation, now known as Del Monte (a subsidiary of R. J. Reynolds, Inc.), commenced commercial operation through its subsidiary, Philippine Packing Corporation. This, along with contemporaneous investments elsewhere by other Hawaiian pineapple producers such as Libby-McNeill, Libby, and

Dole has been attributed to disease problems, for in the early 1920s the Hawaiian pineapple fields were plagued by pineapple wilt, a disease transmitted by the mealy bug.[1]

The Philippine Packing Corporation (PPC) harvested and canned its first commercial crop in 1930. Initially PPC was able to circumvent the constitutional limit on landholding of 1,024 hectares by setting up homesteaders who claimed the land and then in turn leased the land to the corporation. This system was superceded in 1938, when the National Development Company became the legal holder of the pineapple lands in Bukidnon. Homesteader contracts were canceled, and that same year PPC signed a twenty-five-year operating contract with NDC.[2]

The NDC is a public corporation that was created in 1937 under Commonwealth Act No. 182 for the purpose, among others, of engaging "in commercial, industrial, mining, agricultural and other enterprises which may be necessary or contributory to the economic development of the country or important in the public interest and for this purpose, it may hold public agricultural lands and mineral lands in excess of areas permitted to private corporations, associations, and persons by the Constitution and by the laws of the Philippines. . . ."[3]

On August 18, 1938, the NDC, as lessee of public agricultural lands in the province of Bukidnon, entered into a planting agreement with PPC. Senator Lorenzo Tañada in a speech on the floor of the Philippine Senate in 1964 summarized the important features of this contract as follows:

> 1) the public agricultural lands contemplated to be subject of the planting agreement were about 10,000 hectares. As finally determined later and as stipulated in a supplemental agreement executed between the NDC and the Philippine Packing Corporation on February 6, 1939, the public agricultural lands involved consisted of twelve parcels with an aggregate area of 8,195.08 hectares;

> 2) for a period of 25 years (August 18, 1938 to August 18, 1963), renewable for another period of 25 years upon six months notice, the NDC authorized the Philippine Packing Corporation to exclusively occupy the public agricultural lands the NDC had leased and would lease from the Government, and to use the same for the cultivation, harvesting, and transporting of pineapples or any other agricultural crops;

3) for the occupancy and use of the public agricultural lands, the Philippine Packing Corporation would pay yearly to the NDC an amount equivalent to one peso for each hectare of land covered by the agreement; in addition to this, at the end of the fiscal year, the PPC would determine the tonnage of crops it had harvested and compute the value of the same at 10 pesos per ton of 1000 kilograms in the case of pineapples and at such other value as might be mutually agreed upon in the case of other crops. From the total valuation so computed, the expenses incurred on operating account would be subtracted and the difference thereof, if any, considered profits to be divided equally between the NDC and the PPC; if there were no profits nothing would be divided and the loss from the operation was to be absorbed by the PPC. However, this was not really a loss for PPC because its income was derived not from the raw fruit but from the processed and canned pineapple sales, and the valuation of 10 pesos per ton of pineapples was moreover absurdly low.[4]

In 1956, some seven years early and upon the expressed desire of the PPC to renew the planting agreement for another twenty-five years from its expiry date of August 18, 1963, NDC and the PPC executed a new agreement through August 18, 1988. Certain slight amendments in the agreement meant that instead of paying one peso per hectare annually, PPC's rent would rise to 5 pesos, and then for 1963 to 1988 it would pay 10 pesos per hectare. Also, the valuation of pineapples would be raised from 10 pesos per ton to 30 pesos per ton.[5]

Senator Tañada argued in his speech that the grand effective rental paid by PPC to the NDC for its 8,195 hectares during the period 1958–59 to 1961–62 varied from about 65,000 pesos to 83,000 pesos annually. In other words, the yearly rental was between 8 pesos and 10.4 pesos per hectare. This is incredibly cheap compared with what he considered a conservative rent for cultivated and fertile land in Mindanao—about 500 pesos per hectare.[6] At the time the agreement was renewed in 1956, the exchange rate was two pesos to the U.S. dollar. This rate has now deteriorated to about twenty pesos to the U.S. dollar. In dollar terms, then, inflation has sharply reduced the rent that PPC has had to pay for the use of its land.

A more recent estimate was given to me in 1980 by Luis Villareal, who was a part of Philippine Packing Corporation management for ten years before moving to a position on the agribusiness staff of the Ministry of Agriculture. He said that PPC was paying 100 pesos per hectare per year and profits on the plantation are supposed to be shared, but Del Monte loads up the expenses so there is never any profit on the plantation.[7]

From 1939 until at least 1988, PPC has had clear access to 8,000 hectares of land. The agreement between NDC and PPC does, however, rest on tenuous legal grounds, and its constitutionality has been consistently questioned. The NDC is granted the right under law to engage in agricultural enterprises and to *hold* public agricultural lands in excess of the areas permitted to private corporations. There has been no attempt to change the limit (1,024 hectares) on private landholding. Instead the NDC has been used as a way to circumvent the constitutional limit and to accommodate the needs of large-scale agribusiness corporations.

In the 1970s, at least partly in response to the constitutional questions raised over the lease with the NDC, the PPC resorted to another method of obtaining the land it needed for expansion: the crop producer and grower's agreement. This is a twenty-four-page legal document that carefully protects the interests of the company. That the landowners entering the agreement with PPC have no intention of actually growing pineapples themselves is made clear from the form letter attached to the agreement and addressed to "The General Manager, Philippine Packing Corporation, Bago, Cagayan de Oro City."

> Sir:
> We have just concluded a Crop Producer and Grower's Agreement, which, pursuant to paragraph 7, gives the undersigned the right to plant, grow and harvest crops as agreed for your purpose. Such privilege is advantageous to me, but due to the technical ability involved to grow these crops and the sizable amount of finances and equipment needed, I cannot comply and meet this particular condition. In view of this, I am giving the Company or your representative the absolute authority to take over the entire area as agreed and for you to undertake the clearing of the area of existing fruit trees or other trees, and to plant, grow, harvest and purchase the crops necessary for your purpose.

I am doing this for myself and in behalf of all my heirs, successors-in-interest and assigns for the length of time that our Agreement is in force.

Hoping for your favorable consideration. Thank You.

Yours very truly . . .[8]

Once the landowner signed this agreement, the land was turned over to PPC for a period of ten years. The lease was renewable after that, at the option of the company, for another fifteen years on a crop-to-crop basis.

There are no exact figures on the size of PPC's plantation today. Most probably the original 8,000-hectare lease from the NDC has been supplemented by another 6,000 hectares acquired through the crop producer and grower's agreement.

Many absentee landowners and speculators were more than willing to sign the agreement and turn their land over to PPC. Small farmers and tenants were, for the most part, scared or forced off the land. Under martial law, and with the local government bureaucracy on the side of the company, it was easy enough first to isolate small farmers and then to harass them sufficiently that they would leave. They were not happy to leave, and some actually tried to hold out, but most were bought off with payments for their improvements to the land; or PPC cattle were driven through their fields; or rights of way were cut off by the expanding plantation.[9]

While the small farmers and tenants in the path of PPC's expansion have known substantial hardships, the company has performed excellently. It ranks in the top fifty Philippine corporations. In 1979 the company reported profits of 85,651,000 pesos on sales of 905,254,000 pesos and had a return on equity of 22 percent.[10]

Philippine Packing Corporation remains 99 percent owned by Del Monte and firmly under the control of its parent company. In this respect the term joint venture is a misnomer for the project. Del Monte retains complete ownership and control. The NDC serves as an absentee landlord for the project and receives a small (and apparently declining) rental for the land through its lease and "profit-sharing" arrangements.

Some thirty years after the Del Monte investment, Castle and

Cooke made the second major foreign investment in the Philippine fruit products industry by a modern agribusiness corporation.

Throughout the 1940s and 1950s Hawaiian pineapple growers had nervously watched the growth of foreign competition. By 1959 H. C. Cornuelle, president of the Hawaiian Pineapple Company, reported at the annual stockholder's meeting that "Hawaii's portion of the total world supply of solid pack pineapple has slipped from 75 percent to 57 percent in the last 12 years." Cornuelle also reported that, although the foreign product was frequently inferior to Hawaii's, "it has successfully invaded the market because of its lower price."[11] There was every indication during these years that pineapple produced in the developing countries was going to continue to cut into Hawaii's share of the market in Europe, which was less quality-conscious than the United States. As these countries improved quality through added experience and expanded production, moreover, they were going gradually to erode Hawaii's dominance in the U.S. market.

Several factors convinced Castle and Cooke to invest in the Philippines. Among them were labor costs that were less than one-tenth those of Hawaiian labor and were rising much less rapidly; shipping costs that were competitive with Hawaiian rates to both the United States and Europe; a U.S. tariff on Philippine imports that was low enough to be almost inconsequential; and land costs that were only a fraction of those in Hawaii.

The agreement reached between Dole (the fruit products subsidiary of Castle and Cooke) and the NDC was very similar to that of NDC with Philippine Packing Company. Under terms of the 1963 agreement the NDC agreed to acquire, either by lease or by purchase, suitable and sufficient areas of land in Cotabato and to make the same available to Dole so that the company could establish an integrated agroindustrial venture, growing and processing pineapples and other agricultural crops. As summarized by Senator Tañada, Dole agreed to pay NDC:

1) for land which NDC could not buy but just lease from the owners, only and precisely the same rental the NDC had to pay to the owner— that is even without a service charge collectible by the NDC from Dole;

2) for land purchased and owned by the NDC, a yearly rental equal to the purchase price of the land divided by fifty; and

3) as additional minimum rental for each and every year of the first ten years of the agreement an amount equal to 25 centavos multiplied by the number of tons of pineapples harvested by Dole; 35 centavos per ton for each and every year of the next succeeding 15 years; and not less than 50 centavos but not more than one peso in case the contract is renewed for another 25 years. In no event shall the total additional minimum rental be less than an amount equal to two pesos multiplied by the number of hectares covered by the agreement, or an annual rental of two pesos per hectare.[12]

The agreement with Dole was for twenty-five years, renewable at Dole's option for another twenty-five. As of January 15, 1964, the total area of lands acquired pursuant to the agreement was 5,569.1370 hectares of which 3,528.7467 hectares are titled and 2,040.3860 hectares are untitled but formerly occupied by private individuals. The titled lands were mostly free patents and homestead patents, while the untitled lands were farm lots allocated by the defunct National Land Settlement Administration and the Land Settlement Development Company (LASEDECO). All the lands occupied were held in blocks of under twelve hectares and were mostly held by settlers who had moved to Mindanao under one of the government's resettlement schemes to help implement a program of land reform.[13]

Dole claimed in the 1960s after the plantation was productive that it was paying NDC approximately 63 pesos per hectare. With land rent calculated in gradually devalued pesos, total rent costs have obviously declined. At the time the claim was made, the exchange rate was 3.5 pesos to the dollar; today the rate has eroded to about twenty pesos to the dollar. There are also conflicting estimates of the rental paid per hectare. The *Far Eastern Economic Review* in July 8, 1974, stated that Dole pays only 30 pesos per hectare. The Philippine *Business Day International* of March 3, 1975, places the rate even lower, at 25 pesos per hectare per annum.

As of 1979 Dole had about 10,000 hectares devoted to pineapple production. Of this total the company leases 8,000 hectares from the NDC. The remaining 2,000 hectares have been obtained through a farm management contract arrangement. Under the terms of this contract between Dole and individual farmers, the company can use the land for ten years with a renewal option. The Dole Farm Management Contract is similar to the Del Monte Crop Producer and Grower's Agreement. The landowner does not actually produce pineapple but turns the land over to the corporation for a fixed annual rental or lease.

Despite the passage of thirty years between Del Monte's investment and Dole's, the two contracts with the NDC are almost identical. It would seem natural for experience with Del Monte to lead the government to seek contractual arrangements that would guarantee a better return for the land it leased to the company. Dole's investment, however, was made during the administration of President Diosdado Macapagal. He had been elected with strong support from the agricultural exporters, who expected him to lift import and exchange controls that were penalizing the exporters. Much of the president's plan for stimulating economic growth was pinned on increasing agricultural exports, and one way to do this was to attract foreign investors willing to engage in agricultural production for export. To a large degree, therefore, the interests of Dole, including its need for a Third World production platform, and the interests of the Macapagal administration coincided. The result was a lease agreement that was very favorable for Dole.

Dole's investment has been highly successful. The plantation has expanded and the cannery is one of the world's most advanced. In 1979 Dole ranked sixty-third among the top thousand corporations in the Philippines, reporting a net income of 26,915,000 pesos on sales of 355,801,000 pesos and a return on equity of 25 percent.[14]

The next wave of foreign investment in agricultural exports was in bananas. The Philippines started to grow bananas for export in 1967, primarily in response to the liberalization of the tariff on the fruit in the Japanese market. From an initial shipment of 357,783 kilos in 1968, banana exports rose to 23,320,000 kilos the following year when the first plantations became fully operational. From 1969 to 1975, the industry registered an average annual increase of 533.12 percent in exports. This phenomenal growth made it, by 1975, the country's number six earner of foreign currency. Dependence on the Japanese market has, however, always been the hallmark of this industry, and the Philippine share in the Japanese market for bananas rose to 88.1 percent by 1978. Market saturation has forced banana exporters to begin a less than fully successful attempt to diversify into Middle Eastern markets.[15]

There are three multinational corporations active in Mindanao: United Brands (formerly United Fruits), Del Monte, and Dole (through its subsidiary STANFILCO). A fourth multinational, Sumitomo of Japan, has a marketing arrangement with what are nominally independent banana growers. Except for a few hundred hectares that STANFILCO has leased from the NDC and uses to produce bananas, the transnationals all operate through Filipino corporate growers. Table 4.1 gives a breakdown of the affiliation of these corporate growers.

The single most important difference between the pineapple industry and the banana industry is in the acquisition and control of land. Bananas require fertile land in areas subject neither to flooding nor to typhoons. In the Philippines only the southern portion of the island of Mindanao fits these requirements. Unfortunately for the banana companies most of this land was already settled by homesteaders or was being used for the production of abacá (hemp), which made it almost impossible for the NDC to serve as intermediary in the acquisition of land.

Besides the presence of large numbers of settlers on the land most appropriate for banana production, political opposition in the Senate, led by Lorenzo Tañada, made it difficult yet again to turn over thousands of hectares of land to foreign agribusiness corporations. It was this political opposition which put a stop to the plan of United Fruit Company, through its subsidiary the Mindanao Fruit Company, to acquire about 7,000 hectares of the Davao Penal Colony in 1965 to produce pineapples.[16]

The first company to answer the land question was STANFILCO (Standard Philippines Company). STANFILCO was in the mid-sixties owned 66 percent by Dole and 33 percent by a Filipino company, House of Investments. STANFILCO solved the land problem by convincing small farmers in the General Santos area of Cotabato province, near the Dole pineapple plantation, to enter a memorandum agreement, also known as a grower's contract. This program began in 1966 and was followed by expansion into the province of Davao del Norte, also using grower's contracts.

The agreement stipulates that the grower shall grow only the recommended variety of bananas, that company-prescribed agri-

Table 4.1. Corporate banana growers in the Philippines, 1980

	Area planted to bananas (1980)	Number of employees	Banana exports, number of cartons[a] (1979)
Del Monte Growers			
AMS Farming Corp.	949	1,120	3,001,374
Delta Farms, Inc.	420	660	1,081,172
Evergreen Farms, Inc.	532	650[b]	1,501,391
F. S. Dizon & Sons, Inc.	497	430	787,160
Farmington Agro-Development, Inc.	511	663	1,787,204
Hijo Plantation, Inc.	1,595	2,339	4,267,388
Lapanday Agricultural & Dev. Corp.	575	1,716[c]	3,469,042
Marsman Estate Plantation	1,200	1,298	3,935,846
Nova Vista Management Dev. Corp.	108	192	522,969
Standard Fruit Corporation			
Checkered Farms	1,008	1,230	
Golden Farms	1,024	813	17,503,751
Diamond Farms	600	604	
STANFILCO Farms/Small Growers	4,084	3,976	
United Fruits Company			
Tagum Agricultural Dev. Co., Inc.	5,535	6,940	19,146,024
"Independent" Growers			
Davao Fruits Corp.	3,516	3,311	7,075,796
Desidal Fruits Enterprises	907	1,032	2,093,077
Twin Rivers Plantation, Inc.	1,000	1,167	2,385,016
Mabuhay Agricultural Corp.	414	—	—
Mt. Apo Fruits	207	88	234,828
Calinan Agro-Cev., Inc.	195	—	80,891
Soriano Fruits Corp.	230	218	767,840
SEI-Agricultural Dev. Corp.	176	202	287,782
Guihing Agricultural Dev. Corp.	120	—	—

[a]One carton contains 12 kilograms of bananas.
[b]Estimate.
[c]Including Calinan Agro-Dev., Inc., and Guihing Agro-Dev. Corp.
SOURCE. Appendixes 1, 3, and 4 of Randolf S. David et al., *Transnational Corporations and the Philippine Banana Export Industry* (Quezon City: Third World Studies Program, University of the Philippines, 1981).

cultural practices shall be followed, and that the company shall be responsible for irrigation, fertilizer, disease and pest control, harvesting, and packaging the bananas. The company pays for the bananas on a per-box basis. The company's proportionate share of its advances to the grower for irrigation and disease control, and all other advances or other costs incurred by the company on behalf of the grower, are deducted from the gross price of the grower's bananas before the grower receives payment. What the grower actually receives, therefore, is the difference between the gross price of his bananas and the company's deductions.[17]

The STANFILCO program to attract small growers has been reasonably successful. By 1980 there were some 368 small growers who devoted 2,628 hectares to the production of bananas.[18] Measured in terms of indebtedness, however, the program has not been equally successful for the small grower. Randolph David and his colleagues report that in the Davao area the average indebtedness of the small grower to the company is 7,048 pesos per hectare.[19]

STANFILCO also has three much larger corporate growers. These are Checkered Farms (1,008 hectares), Golden Farms (1,024 hectares), and Diamond Farms (600 hectares). The relations between company and corporate grower are very similar to those of Del Monte and its corporate growers—a subject to be discussed below.

But before turning to Del Monte we look at the joint venture between United Fruits and the Tagum Agricultural Development Corporation (TADECO). TADECO was owned by Antonio Floirendo, the most prominent businessman of Southern Mindanao and a close political friend of both presidents Macapagal and Marcos. Floirendo, who has now fled the country, was once described as a man who could work with whatever politician was in power and as the warlord for Region XI, the Davao region. He was said to have been "the errand boy for Macapagal." And for many years he had a great deal of power because of his closeness to President Marcos. One banana industry insider remarked in 1980 that "it is not as in the pre–martial law days when a warlord still had to work hard to maintain his hierarchy of supporters and deliver the pork barrel goodies. Now he is under no pressure to deliver to anyone except Marcos."[20]

TADECO began in 1950 when Floirendo was able to purchase 1,024 hectares of the Davao Penal Colony. This area was developed and planted to abacá. Initially very profitable, the production of abacá became a basis for Floirendo's expansion into a number of other businesses. He became, for example, the Davao region distributor for Ford Motor cars and trucks. In the mid-1960s, however, world demand for abacá dropped as synthetic products began to replace those made of hemp.

By this time Floirendo was going into debt because, presumably, of losses on abacá.[21] At the same time, having failed in its attempt to lease land from the Davao Penal Colony, United Fruits was still looking for a way to acquire land in the Davao region. Ultimately, Antonio Floirendo and United Fruits got together. The result was a marketing contract that assured TADECO of the sale of its fruits in Japan for twenty years. Floirendo immediately began converting abacá lands to the production of bananas. He also began to accumulate land.

Floirendo carried out his expansion in several ways. Some of the land was bought from small farmers, some was leased. There are numerous reports that, as in the expansion of the pineapple plantation, TADECO, in buying and leasing the lands of small farmers, often resorted to harassment and intimidation. Rumors say that the company was never reluctant to make use of the military, police, and Civilian Home Defense Forces to enforce its wishes.[22]

Most of TADECO's land, however, was acquired through its 1969 "plantation development agreement" with the Bureau of Prisons. Under the terms of the agreement TADECO, at its own expense, would undertake to clear and develop into a banana plantation "certain parcels" of land owned by the bureau. These are the very same lands in the Davao Penal Colony which were denied to United Fruits in 1964 because of political opposition.

According to TADECO executives, the agreement allows TADECO to make use of Davao Penal Colony lands on condition that the company employ prison labor in connection with the penal colony's "rehabilitation program." In 1980 it was estimated that TADECO occupied at least 4,420 hectares of Penal Colony land on which it paid a rental or lease fixed since 1969 at 250 pesos per hectare per year, plus ten centavos for every box of bananas produced by the company.[23] TADECO's total plantation area in 1981 was about 5,535 hectares.

The Del Monte Corporation has found a similar way to acquire banana lands. Del Monte, through its wholly owned subsidiary, the Philippine Packing Corporation (PPC), started its banana export operations in 1968. It has growing and marketing contracts with nine corporate farms in the Davao provinces. At the start of the 1980s it also entered into a production and marketing contract with a newly opened corporate banana farm in Misamis Oriental province.

Del Monte's control over its corporate growers in all key phases of the banana export industry is formalized in three basic contracts with its growers: the Production and Purchase Agreement, the Technical Services Agreement, and the Real Property Improvement and Production Loan Agreement. The Production and Purchase Agreement is a contract between the corporate grower and Del Monte International, Inc. The other two agreements are contracts between the corporate grower and the Philippine Packing Corporation. For purposes of the contracts, PPC is designated by Del Monte as the "services company" whose "agricultural know-how and technical services" the growers agree to engage for the duration of the contract.

The Production and Purchase Agreement is basically a contract between the grower and Del Monte wherein the grower agrees to grow and sell giant cavendish bananas exclusively to Del Monte, except under circumstances expressly allowed by Del Monte's prior written approval. In short, Del Monte has the first right to everything that the growers can produce. In return for this exclusivity the grower receives a minimum purchase price guaranteed to cover the grower's necessary costs plus profits. This agreement is for a minimum of ten years with either of the parties enjoying the absolute right to extend the contract for an additional five-year period up to a maximum of three such periods, or a total of twenty-five years.[24]

The most obvious point of tension between the growers and Del Monte is the purchase price of bananas. During July of 1980 the corporate growers and Del Monte were negotiating over a raise in the purchase price, which they can do whenever they can show there has been a 10 percent increase in the cost of production. They were, however, getting the "run around" from Del Monte officials.[25] They were also renegotiating the general terms of their various agreements preparatory to renewing them, because the original ten-year agreements were about to expire.

The growers were seeking a 20 percent return on the cost of production (about 40,000 pesos per hectare) and a 22 percent profit, which worked out to about $1.95 per box of bananas produced. Del Monte was offering a 15 percent return on overhead and a 15 percent profit, or about $1.50 per box.[26]

The hard-nose bargaining style of Del Monte coupled with the saturation and subsequent decline in prices for the Japanese market has meant hard times for the Del Monte corporate growers. Throughout the early 1980s Del Monte was forced to take over the management or, in a few cases, buy out the interests of local banana growers.[27] There is also said to be a difference in corporate styles between Del Monte and Dole. According to one man interviewed, "Dole gives out loans to its growers, keeps the plantations going and perpetually in debt. Del Monte drives a hard bargain and transfers any losses to its growers."[28]

The final group of banana growers are the "independents," which range in size from the 120 hectares of the Guihing Agricultural Development Corporation to the 3,516 hectares of the Davao Fruits Corporation. Some of these corporations have Japanese investments; almost all have some formal marketing arrangement with a Japanese corporation. With declining prices in the Japanese market, these companies have suffered as much as or more than other banana growers. They do not, for the most part, have the resources of a big multinational corporation to fall back on. When faced with economic difficulties, these growers cut back on expenses by not paying workers. If conditions remain poor they can be forced to sell their land.

The third wave of multinational interest in Philippine agriculture began in the late 1970s. In October 1979 President Marcos issued Presidential Decree No. 1648 "Reorganizing the National Development Company and Establishing a Revised Charter Therefor." Besides raising the capitalization of the NDC from 450 million pesos to 10 billion pesos, the new decree reiterated and strengthened the role of the NDC in acquiring land for plantation projects. Section 4 of the decree outlines the powers and functions of the company. There are several points under section 4 which deal specifically with the question of land. In particular the company can

2) Hold public agricultural lands and mineral lands in excess of the areas permitted to private corporations, associations and persons by the Constitution and by the laws of the Philippines;

4) Make contracts and enter into such arrangements as it may consider convenient and advantageous to its interests, for the development, exploitation, and operation of any of its land or mineral holdings, as well as of its industrial enterprises;

14) Exercise the right of eminent domain as may be necessary for the purpose for which the Company is created;

17) Hold public lands, including logged over areas, which the President may allocate for specific projects of the Company.

In addition to these points, Section 5—Public Lands Availability—states that "upon certification by the President, for priority projects of the Company, the Bureau of Lands and the Bureau of Forestry shall make available without delay the necessary public land to undertake such priority projects. The aforesaid priority projects, specifically agricultural plantation projects, which are certified as such by the President, shall have preferential rights over logged over areas, the provisions of Presidential Decree 705 notwithstanding."

The last chairman of the board for the NDC under Marcos, Minister of Industry Roberto Ongpin, in commenting on the measures contained in PD 1648 spoke directly to the issue of plantation agriculture. The NDC, he said, "will also promote plantation agriculture which holds tremendous potential in generating employment and export capabilities." Also the NDC, "being a government entity, can hold lands larger than what is normally allowed of private corporations and it would take advantage of this by directly or indirectly engaging in plantation agriculture, raising export crops such as palm, cacao, soybeans, and rubber."[29] Somewhat later Minister Ongpin again stressed the importance of the NDC for plantation agriculture when he pointed out that "one thousand hectares would not be viable for a plantation. That is why we have NDC—to get around the constitutional limit."[30]

Within a few months of the signing of Presidential Decree 1648, several major new plantation projects were announced. These were all joint-venture projects between the NDC and foreign, primarily Malaysian-based, multinational corporations. In some instances private Filipino investors contributed a small portion of the capital for these projects.

From newspaper accounts we can discern the new projects in broad outline. The first investment, for a palm oil project, came from the Malaysian-based but at the time British-owned Guthrie Holdings. On February 4, 1980, Guthrie signed a joint-venture agreement with NDC to develop 8,000 hectares in logging concessions in Agusan del Sur province. Guthrie will own 40 percent of the 400-million-peso subsidiary, which will be known as NDC-Guthrie Plantations, Inc. (NGPI). NDC will own the land while Guthrie will provide the capital and expertise, for which it will receive a management fee. In addition to the plantation, Guthrie will also put up a crushing mill that will employ thirty workers. A total of slightly under three thousand workers will be hired once the plantation complex is fully developed, in 1988.[31]

On May 30, 1980, a second palm oil venture was finalized with the signing of an agreement between Dunlop International Ltd., a subsidiary of Dunlop Holdings of England, and NDC for the cultivation of 5,000 hectares, also in Agusan del Sur. Dunlop's Filipino partner is Oliverio Laperal who will own 5 percent of the total equity of 300 million pesos. Dunlop will own 30–40 percent while NDC will hold 55–65 percent. Dunlop will also set up a processing mill in its plantation.[32]

On July 25, 1980, it was announced that a third palm oil project had been signed between NDC, Keck Seng(M) Berhad (another Malaysian corporation), and a group of Filipinos led by Leonardo Ty. The venture, called Agusan Plantations, Inc., was planned for an initial 8,000 hectares with an option to expand by 12,000 hectares after three years. Keck Seng was to absorb 40 percent of the initial capitalization of 400 million pesos and NDC would own 10 percent, while the Ty group, already part-owners of the giant Manila Paper Mills in Agusan, was to take 50 percent of the equity. (The project never materialized. Like many others it was killed by the collapse of the Philippine economy and growing political instability.)[33]

At least two other groups negotiated with the NDC during the Marcos years for leases of large blocs of land for plantations: Sime Darby Berhad sought 8,000 hectares in Agusan;[34] and a joint venture consisting of Boustead and Company of Malaysia and Singapore, the United Overseas Bank of Singapore, the Filinvest Development Corporation, and another Filipino firm known as Interco was reported to be interested in a 10,000-hectare plantation for palm oil.[35]

If newspaper accounts were correct, then, some 33,000 hectares were set aside in Agusan del Sur province and 26,000 hectares more were being eyed for giant palm oil plantations. As of mid-1980 a total of 1.1 billion pesos had beem committed to develop an initial 21,000 hectares of plantation land.

Of all these projects the one that had progressed the furthest was the NDC-Guthrie joint venture known as NGPI. In support of NGPI President Marcos issued Proclamation Number 1939, "Establishing as National Development Company Reservation for Agricultural Plantation Cultivation the Parcel of Land of the Public Domain Situated in the Provinces of Agusan and Surigao, Island of Mindanao," on January 22, 1980. By means of this proclamation President Marcos did "withdraw from sale, settlement, exploration or exploitation and set aside and reserve for the use of the National Development Company for agricultural plantation cultivation," two parcels of land—one parcel of approximately 11,200 hectares and a second of approximately 17,500 hectares.

The proclamation implies that this is an unpopulated area just recently cleared of its forest cover and thus ready for unencumbered development by NGPI. Government officials could have been simply ignorant of the true situation. Officials of both the National Development Company and the Board of Investments told me that the land slated for plantation development was "newly logged over" and "unsettled."[36] Even NGPI stated that the company would over the next six years be "responsible for clearing an area of *rain forest* in the general region of San Francisco, Agusan del Sur."[37] But even a single trip to the barrios located in the path of this project, and I made several trips, would highlight the number of settlers involved and the magnitude of the problems generated by these new developments.

Two barrios of Rosario town in Agusan del Sur—Mate and Cabantao—as well as a small cluster of houses known as sito Maligaya, are located within the boundaries of the first phase of NGPI plantation. These communities were inhabited by, respectively, 300, 80, and 60 *families,* a mixture of native families and Christian settlers. Very few, if any, of the families in the area have been able to get title to their land, even though many have been trying for the last five to ten years. The farmers reported that sometime in the early 1960s the land they now occupy, formerly the CBL logging concession, was approved by the Bureau of Forestry for release to settlers. In 1971 an area of at least 1,300 hectares, including sito Maligaya, was released after being surveyed. But in 1972, following the declaration of martial law, the survey was annulled, and the area was once again declared public land. Despite the best efforts of the settlers, they remain squatters on land they have struggled long, hard years to clear and make productive. Now, with PD 1939 in January 1980, two parcels of the CBL logging concession totaling 28,700 hectares have been turned over to the NDC by presidential proclamation. Local government officials have seen copies of this proclamation, but the settlers have not, nor were they consulted before it was issued.[38]

In this particular case the foreign investor and manager of the joint venture, Guthrie Overseas Holding Ltd., tried to work its way out of a difficult and unexpected situation. Guthrie had been promised a tract of forest land without a settler problem.[39] The management officials, with the strong support of the officer-in-charge at the local branch of the Philippine National Bank (also serving as a labor contractor for the project), the minister from the local Protestant church, officials from the Luis Taruc–led FAITH (Federation of Agrarian and Industrial Toiling Hands), and the Presidential Assistant for National Minorities canvassed the area. They promised the settlers that if they gave up their land, they would receive employment at a minimum wage of 550 pesos per month, plus free housing, electricity, and water, plus minimal compensation for improvements that the settlers had made to the land.

For a number of reasons, including the fact that the military and a paramilitary group known as the Lost Command were active in the area and forced some relocation of settlers, some farmers renounced their claims to the land.[40] Many, however, resisted the pressure to relinquish their land and asked questions like "How much can 550 pesos buy at this time?" and "Aren't your promises sugar-coated?" In response to the promise made by FAITH that it will give five hectares to each settler who loses his land, the settlers have asked, "Where will this five hectares be, in the marsh?" These questions represent a healthy skepticism on the part of the settlers and, probably, an intuitive knowledge that holding on to their land affords them a better future than leasing it to the plantation, as small farmers have done in the banana- and pineapple-growing areas. And working as a daily laborer at 550 pesos per month is not very attractive to settlers who can make a free choice.

Summary

Bananas, pineapples, and palm oil are all produced by multinational corporations in the Philippines for the world market. The multinationals bring to the Philippines their brand names and their markets, as well as a limited amount of capital and technology.

These factors alone would make the MNCs important economic actors capable of defending their interests against an aggressive political leader such as Ferdinand Marcos. The MNCs, however, have also had the assistance of powerful allies inside the Philippines. In the production of bananas, for example, the multinationals have worked closely with large Filipino landlords—landlords who, on their own, are also politically powerful. Within the state (that is, within the administrative apparatus of the state), there have also been ardent supporters of MNC investment in agriculture. Officials within the Ministry of Agriculture, the National Economic and Development Authority, and the Board of Investments have almost uniformly advocated special privileges and incentives for foreign investors.

Two key factors have strengthened the hand of the foreign investor. Unlike in sugar and coconuts, the entire fruit products industry is dominated by MNCs. There is no commodity market for products such as pineapples, which gives the multinational corporations a power internationally that also has implications for the domestic political economy. In sugar and coconuts the private sector depends on the state administrative apparatus, in particular the technocrats, to defend it against the predations of the politicians. The multinationals also depend on these technocrats, but in the fruit products industry there is less dependence and more of an active joint effort to insulate the private sector from political manipulation.

The combined strength of multinational investor, state technocrat, and big landlord was sufficient to protect this industry from most political manipulation during martial law. It has also been strong enough to help shape the Philippine political economy. I address the issue of the role of the Philippines in the international political economy in the concluding chapter, but here it is important to emphasize the impact of MNC agribusiness investment on two key factors in the domestic political economy—land and labor.

The land frontier in the Philippines is closed. In both pineapples and bananas the initial establishment of plantations was relatively easy compared with the costs of expansion in the 1970s. At first large and small landholders alike were attracted by lump sum payments of several years' lease rentals or promises of easy money from contract growing. In the 1970s, as the plantations expanded to meet rising world demand, they pushed outward against small landholders who did not want to lease their land. These landholders saw that earlier promises had not been completely true. In response the military powers of the martial law government, subterfuge by government officials in the Bureau of Land cooperating with absentee landlords, harassment, and intimidation by corporate officials have all been used to get rid of the smallholders and acquire land needed for expansion. The Marcos government was a willing partner in clearing the way for the plantations. It canceled old land surveys that would have allowed settlers to obtain title to their plots. Local government officials were active in trying to convince settlers to give up their land. Because the government, through the National Development Corporation, was a partner in the latest plantations, it spared no effort to make the venture succeed.

The record under Marcos suggests an important lesson for the Aquino government. It may be difficult to remain loyal to democratic principles while at the same time preparing the way for new foreign investment in plantation agribusiness.

The second issue is labor. There are roughly thirty thousand workers in the banana and pineapple industries and a growing number of workers in other, newer crops. Under Marcos, workers were not free to organize their own independent unions. For the most part they received the legally mandated minimum daily wage, and many did not even receive the legal minimum. These wage levels are insufficient to meet the minimum daily nutritional requirements of workers' families. As a consequence the health, educational, and housing needs of workers and their families have suffered severely.

In reponse to these problems many workers I talked with said they had given up hope of ever getting good wages or a strong union. Instead they were mobilizing to support or were joining the fight of the New People's Army. These same workers were the people who, in the provinces, supported Aquino's successful campaign to oust Marcos. Having supported Aquino, these workers hope to see some improvement in their lives. Their aspirations, however, will not be easy to meet, for what they need are higher wages and, most important, land—workers whose identities I may not reveal told me that they dreamed of the day when they could take their machetes and chop down the banana plants and begin growing corn.

The multinational corporations seek a safe environment in which to invest. In the Philippine context this has sometimes meant that they must enter joint-venture projects with the government. The government, in turn, seeks greater revenues from agricultural exports, for which it must rely on the multinationals for their expertise and their markets. This complementarity of interests has changed little during the twentieth century. As various factors of production have become scarce—most notably land—so the power of the government has increased somewhat, but the basic complementarity of interests remains the same, at the very least for crops where a handful of MNCs controls the market and technical expertise.

The multinational corporations and their local allies, unlike the landlords in sugar and coconuts, did not represent a domestic political threat to Marcos. This, too, increased the willingness of the two partners to cooperate. Under Corazon Aquino's government, the complementarity of interests continues. Those left out—the small landholders and the workers—will most likely continue to suffer until more dramatic changes take place in the Philippine political economy. Such changes will have to come at the level of the state. It is to this issue, the political economy of the Philippine state, that we now turn.

Chapter Five

State and Regime in the Philippine Context

The preceding three chapters have discussed the impact of recent changes in the Philippines on the country's major agricultural export industries. There are several conclusions we can draw from these findings regarding the role these industries play in the modern political economy. We can also use our findings as a foundation for a broader discussion of Philippine politics, both domestically and in international comparison, but this requires that we go beyond the agricultural export industries to other sectors of the political economy. It also requires an elaboration of the role that the Philippines plays in the world economy.

From the case studies we can draw several initial generalizations:

1) One of the most significant effects of the colonization of the Philippines was the creation of an agrarian elite. This elite dominated regional and local politics and, for much of the twentieth century, was largely autonomous from centralized, national political control.

2) The agrarian elite that dominated Philippine politics had its economic foundation in production for the U.S. market. The agricultural export economy was dependent on the U.S. market because it developed in a colonial context. Philippine products entered the United States free of duty; as a consequence of this favored position, at least in the case of sugar, the country failed to develop the ability to compete on the international market. Dependence on the U.S. market shaped the nature of the struggle for

political independence, and since independence it has distorted national development planning.

3) Diversification of the Philippine economy after World War II, especially during the period of import-substitution industrialization in the 1950s, resulted in a decline in elite cohesion, an upsurge of popular political participation and nationalism, and a continuation of trends toward a stronger central government with greater control over economic resources.

4) The breakdown of elite cohesion, the economic decline of the late 1960s, and the growing sense of nationalism in large segments of the population led many to question the legitimacy of the political system and the continued rule of an elite led by President Ferdinand Marcos.

5) Attempts by Marcos to solidify his rule and to lead the nation toward a more open economy, in which foreign investment would play a larger role, failed. They were stymied by a combination of factors, including an entrenched group of import-substitution manufacturers, the growing nationalist reaction to foreign domination of the Philippine economy, and the continued power of rural elites who were reluctant to allow any further centralization of power, especially in the hands of a lame-duck president whose term of office was scheduled to end on December 31, 1973.

AGRICULTURAL EXPORT INDUSTRIES AND THE
TRANSFORMATION OF THE POLITICAL ECONOMY

With the declaration of martial law on September 21, 1972, Marcos was able to act against sectors of society which challenged the legitimacy of elite rule and his own continuation in office. The entrenched interests of manufacturers for the domestic market came under sustained attack; tariffs were lowered, the currency was devalued, and incentives or subsidies for consumption were progressively removed. Other groups had their rights curtailed: nationalists, students, militant unionists, and opposition political figures. In the Philippines the political sphere had expanded during the 1950s and 1960s, and so the transition to export-led industrialization there differed from that in South Korea or in Taiwan. Depoliticization was swift and widespread under martial law; in each case, however, groups sought to delay the transformation, they resisted disenfranchisement, and they found new ways to affect the political process.

The power of the agricultural exporters in sugar and coconuts was sharply circumscribed. The institutions that had long expressed the exporters' political interests—the Congress and the political parties in particular—were either disbanded or carefully monitored and regulated. In addition, the private armies of regional politicians were disbanded, and the government confiscated hundreds of thousands of firearms in the hands of private citizens. Many opposition mayors and governors were replaced by presidential decree. Occasionally individual families were singled out and made an example so that others might see what fate awaited those deemed to be enemies of the president. The Lopez family— one of the richest in the country, its wealth originally based on sugar but since diversified—was among those singled out for special treatment. The family's media empire was taken over by Roberto Benedicto, a long time presidential friend, adviser, and campaign treasurer. The family's electrical generation plants, which supplied most of the electricity for Manila, were taken over by First Philippine Holding Company—believed to have been a vehicle for the investment interests of the family of Imelda Romualdez Marcos.[1]

The more significant way to weaken the agricultural elites, however, was to create monopolies to control the export of coconuts and sugar, place these monopolies firmly under the control of presidential friends, and use the monopolies as a vehicle to accumulate surplus at the national level rather than at the regional level. As Hermenegildo Zayco, a governor of the Board of Investments, said to me in 1980, "in a developing country like the Philippines which is semi-totalitarian, it is necessary for the President to have essential sectors of the economy in his control, or in the control of his trusted associates. This is what has happened with Philsucom [Philippine Sugar Commission] and Unicom [United Coconut Oil Mills, Inc.]."[2]

Marcos used the agricultural export sector as a foundation for his regime. He skillfully assembled the parts of a new coalition that lasted as long as commodity prices remained high and the economy continued to grow. He started by replacing local officials who opposed him personally and eliminating the Congress, an institution that could have opposed his subsequent manipulation of the agroexport industries. Having consolidated his political control, he then placed Benedicto in charge of trading sugar. He used a presidential decree to form this government monopoly, and so what Marcos formed was, at least nominally, a state trading monopoly— something common to commodity exporters in both First and Third Worlds. In the Philippines, though, the state monopoly was used for largely private ends. Surplus from the sugar industry was accumulated at the national level—at the expense of workers, planters, and millers. There has not yet been, and there may never be, an accurate accounting of the final disposition of the surplus generated in sugar. By the early 1980s the industry was in financial ruin, with massive unemployment and hunger among the workers. It is safe to say that the vast bulk of the surplus generated went not to reinvestment in the industry but rather to the personal and political needs of the First Family. Much of the capital was taken out of the country.

In coconuts a similar trading (and milling) monopoly was established. But in this case presidential decrees were used to establish what was legally a private monopoly held by presidential associates in the name of the coconut farmers. The surplus was centralized just as in sugar. It was controlled by a presidential crony, Eduardo Cojuangco, Jr., who was joined in this venture by the minister of national defense, Juan Ponce Enrile.

It is not entirely accurate to call what happened in these two industries the creation of a state monopoly or a private monopoly. In one case, sugar was a state monopoly, but the surplus did not go to the state. In the other, coconuts were a private monopoly where the surplus did not go to the private sector. Here I call them quasi state monopolies to connote the use of state power to benefit not the state itself but the chosen few of the Marcos regime.

Obviously in the fruit products industry, where multinational investment was dominant, Marcos could not use the same tactics. In bananas he was able to establish through preferential political action the position of Antonio Floirendo, another close associate. However, the multinational banana and pineapple companies could resist the partisan political manipulation of Marcos the more easily because their legal access to land was long settled and their control over markets, technology, and capital was secure. In the newer investments in palm oil, it seems, the strength of the state was used to assure a place for state participation in the ventures, but opportunities for political manipulation were still more limited than in sugar or coconuts.

Marcos was able to build a political coalition out of such blatant favoritism for several good reasons. First, every politician retained office only at the pleasure of Marcos. Second, entrepreneurship has always been politicized in the Philippines. Past profits relied on getting political support for a sugar quota in the protected U.S. market, or for an import license, or for special access to government credit. The style of doing business was no different after martial law, it was just that political power was more concentrated. Planters and millers still made some money—partly by squeezing their workers even harder—and they saw the key to greater profitability not in getting rid of Marcos but in getting close to Marcos. Politicians, landowners, planters, and millers found themselves dependent on Marcos for their future. It is important to remember that the Philippine Sugar Commission controlled prices of sugar, and access to credit, and legal wage levels. Both political office and profitability required acquiescence to, if not active support of, the Marcos presidency. In turn, through his control over the elite, Marcos sought to manipulate election returns to his own benefit.

Within the agroexport industries Marcos based his political coalition more on the pursuit of individual interest than on commitment to an ideology or even a shared vision of how agricultural exports could lead to national development. In the fruit products sector the multinational corporations wanted to be free to pursue profit, and Marcos left them to pursue these private interests. To this end they received easy access to land, a docile and disciplined labor force, and little government interference. In return Marcos had direct and indirect support from the multinationals. In the coconut and sugar sectors the picture is more complex, because it involves the nature of the Filipino landowning elite. Members of the elite have always been conservative; their position in society has always rested on privilege and great inequality. As a result the elite had no firm societal base from which to oppose Marcos. Their wealth was being siphoned off, and they had lost their institutional bases of political power. Most of the planters and millers thus chose to support Marcos and his political party, the New Society Movement (Kilusang Bagong Lipunan or KBL), in spite of whatever they might have felt personally. For them it was too risky in the early years of martial law to challenge Marcos. They knew he could impose land reform; they knew what had happened to colleagues who were his old political enemies. The elite acquiesced and collaborated, just as the elite had acquiesced and collaborated with the Spanish and the Americans long before Marcos came to power. The support for Marcos among the elite in the agroexport sector was one of the major props for the regime. In return for elite support Marcos did not challenge continued class rule in the countryside. He chose to rule from the top down and never did develop a political party with a large mass base, but he did draw strong regional political leadership from the agroexport industries. Roberto Benedicto of the sugar industry was regional director of the KBL party for Region VII, the major sugar-producing region. From the coconut industry Marcos drew Eduardo Cojuangco, Jr., KBL regional director for the politically vital Central Luzon region, and Juan Ponce Enrile, regional director of the Cagayan Valley, Region II. From the banana industry came Antonio Floirendo, regional director for the KBL for the southern portion of the island of Mindanao. Such men and their political supporters received tremendous economic privilege by presidential decree, and in return they were called upon to mobilize local and regional support for Marcos. The system worked for most of a decade, and it was acceptable to many, perhaps a majority, during the early years of martial law. Bureaucratic reforms, increased rice production, land reform, new inflows of foreign investment, and high commodity prices combined to give President Marcos a measure of legitimacy and popularity.

Our three case studies also illustrate that Ferdinand Marcos was hardly the typical "modern" authoritarian ruler. He was quick to justify his rule in terms of rational, centralized planning for economic development. But what we actually find is a consistent pattern of political manipulation of the agroexport industries, creating a personalized rule based in the final analysis on military repression. Despite the early promise of reform, that rule was as corrupt and inefficient as in any other regime in the contemporary world.

At its core the Marcos regime had the support of those personally loyal to him, although their loyalty depended in most cases on
the continued freedom to earn monopolistic privilege. When Marcos began to falter, their loyalty began to wane. The repressive
machinery—the military and police—supported Marcos; they
were his chosen instrument of political control, and as a consequence their power and earnings had increased dramatically. Local
politicians were totally dependent on their ability to remain in the
personal favor of Marcos, and so they too were loyal as long as
Marcos was in full control.

However, if we move from the Marcos regime and its support to
what the fourteen years of authoritarianism represented at a more
structural level, at the level of the state, we see a somewhat different picture emerging.

THE ROLE OF THE STATE

For the Philippines there can be no denying that the state expresses "a situation of domination" and reflects the interests of
dominant classes. The agricultural export industries abound in
examples of state power being used to further class domination.
The creation under colonialism of a system of land ownership and
the protection of the rights of private property embedded in that
ownership by the state's legal and coercive organizations have been
important to the growing concentration of wealth in the countryside and to the numerous peasant uprisings of the nineteenth
and twentieth centuries.

One of the state's administrative organizations, the National Development Company, was of central importance in the dispossess-
sion of small settlers and landowners who occupied areas that multinational agribusiness corporations had chosen for the production
of pineapples, bananas, palm oil, rubber, and a number of lesser
crops. Where small farmers stood in the way of the dominant class
of foreign investors and their local joint-venture partners, as we
have seen, the coercive organizations of the state were used to
intimidate the smallholders or to force them into leaving.

In the coconut and sugar industries also it is the state that has
determined wage levels and working conditions, as well as the ex-

tent to which social welfare programs should be extended to the countryside. The class nature of the state means that the largely unorganized workers in these two industries have been left to fend for themselves in opposition to the interests of the owners of plantations and processing plants. As a result wages are so low that the families of workers in the sugar and coconut industries are among the most poverty-stricken in the nation and also make up a disproportionate share of the malnourished.

In 1979 the World Bank prepared a confidential, 392-page report on poverty in the Philippines. The report documents a sharp decline in real wages since the 1960s, and it says purchasing power dropped "in both urban and rural areas, in all regions, and practically all occupations." It found that real wages for skilled laborers in Manila and its suburbs dropped 23.8 percent between 1972 and 1978. The plunge was even more precipitous, 31.6 percent, for unskilled laborers. Other World Bank documents have observed that the rich-poor gap is "worse in the Philippines than elsewhere in the [Southeast Asian] region, and is exceeded only in Latin America."[3]

In a surprisingly frank statement the U.S. Agency for International Development offers an explanation for the widespread poverty of the Philippines. In 1980 it reported that

> the structure of the economy with its heavy reliance on primary agricultural product exports to finance relatively capital-intensive industrialization and a rising energy bill, undercuts the poor's efforts to survive. . . . Sugar, coconut, banana, and coffee export expansion favors plantation agriculture and ties up substantial land assets in the hands of the few to the detriment of the landless agricultural workers who receive a small share of the returns while suffering prolonged unemployment during periods of oversupply and periodically depressed prices. . . . While the poorer households are the major producers of these primary products, the returns accrue disproportionately to marketing and banking concerns. . . . The skewed income distribution is the outcome of the "invisible hand" of a relatively laissez faire economy that evolved from colonial trade patterns and private investment choices guided by vested interests and supported by the political culture and patronage system.[4]

As a result of the fundamental, structural problems of the Philippine economy, inequality is rising quite rapidly. A report by the

Center for Research and Communication, a business- and church-supported study group in the Philippines, shows that in the midst of extreme poverty the wealthiest 10 percent of all families earned 45 percent of national income in 1981, up from less than 30 percent in 1971. The poorest 70 percent of families, on the other hand, earned just 31 percent of national income in 1981, compared with 48 percent a decade earlier.[5]

Internationally the state used its administrative organizations to protect and enlarge the Philippine sugar quota in the lucrative, protected U.S. market, first the duty-free quota and later, especially after the embargo against Cuban sugar, the absolute quota. Domestically the administrative machinery in the sugar industry was geared almost exclusively to producing sufficient sugar to fill the quota for the U.S. market—limiting production when the quota was easily filled, and stimulating an expansion of the number of sugar mills and the hectarage planted to cane whenever there was any danger that the all-important quota would not be filled.

In these examples it is clear that the Philippine state operates in the interests of the bourgeoisie and against the interests of workers and small landowners. But this generalization requires clarification. In earlier chapters I wrote of an agricultural elite, and it was appropriate to do so in the sense that landowners fulfilled multiple roles in the countryside, political, economic, and social. The elite was in most cases a traditional patron enmeshed in complex yet hierarchical ties that bound elite to workers and tenants. In this chapter, however, it is necessary to begin thinking of the rural elite as a part of a broader class—both rural and urban—which is modern and capitalist, which owns the means of social production, and which increasingly employs wage labor. As this change in terminology implies, the economic role of rural landowners has become more important than the political role they once played, and polarization between classes is increasing. However, it is also clearly incorrect to assert in simplistic fashion that the state operates in the interest of the bourgeoisie, because we know that the "relatively autonomous" state has taken action detrimental to some segments of the bourgeoisie. Each segment, in one useful formulation, has "a relatively distinct location in the social process of production and, consequently, its own specific political economic requirements and concrete interests which may be contradictory to those of other class segments with which, nonetheless, it shares essentially the same relationship to ownership of productive property. As such, a class segment has the inherent potential for developing a specific variant of intraclass consciousness and common action in relation to other segments of the class."[6]

Each capitalist state, in the process of choosing and implementing public policy, responds to the specific political-economic requirements and concrete interests of a number of class segments. The state may use its coercive and administrative organizations to protect the interests of the bourgeoisie as a whole, but it must choose among policies that invariably favor some class segments more than others.

As we sort out the activities of the state in the Philippines, it may be helpful to think of the state's economic actions in the categories proposed by E. V. K. Fitzgerald: support and control.

> The first case, and by far the most common one, is that of an economy where the state acts so as to support accumulation in the private sector, and thus the domestic bourgeoisie, probably in alliance with foreign enterprise. This support takes a number of forms, apart from the maintenance of a certain social structure: the provision of physical infrastructure such as roads; the supply of cheap inputs such as power and steel; the extension of investment finance from development banks; and finally the grant of tariff protection and tax concessions to private enterprise. . . . The state cannot undertake autonomous accumulation. . . .
>
> The second case, in contrast, occurs when the role of the state becomes more independent—by substitution for the domestic bourgeoisie—and an autonomous basis of accumulation is established in state capitalism. Surplus mobilization is centered on the state and the object of investment is not private profit, but the economic development of the economy as a whole.[7]

These categories—state support and state control—are not nearly as mutually exclusive as Fitzgerald implies. The Philippine case suggests that the state can support private capital accumulation while at the same time moving toward greater state control of important sectors of the economy. But what is of greater importance, both practically and theoretically, is that the Philippines suggests a third category. The Marcos regime used the powers of the state to further its own economic and political interests. Marcos did so through investments made by his and his wife's families and through his close political associates and friends, those known in the Philippines as cronies.

There are four separate class segments to which the state responds. One segment is based in the state organizations and supports greater state capitalism. A second segment, the cronies, is largely private but depends on its close ties to the president and seeks to use the powers of the state to advance its own private ends. The third and fourth segments are the rest of the bourgeoisie, divided between those oriented toward production for the domestic market and those oriented toward production for the world market. The internationalized segment includes the agricultural exporters who by the actions of the state have in political terms been largely emasculated, and if the voice of the agricultural exporters was heard under Marcos, it was a voice that supported greater participation in the international economy. There are important differences between the two segments, but this division of the bourgeoisie may be more important analytically than in real life, because many of the major families of the Philippines have economic empires that transcend these analytical categories. Nevertheless there are important and clearly defined political differences that can be identified on the basis of support for particular industrialization policies.

These four groups can be visualized as class segments because each one has specific political-economic requirements and concrete interests. Their concrete interests are in many cases contradictory. Yet all four groups share essentially the same relationship to the ownership of productive property.

Much of Philippine politics on a day-to-day basis appears to be personal and factional infighting, a pursuit of political office for the patronage and power that the office provides to the elected few. At a deeper and therefore less visible level of analysis, Philippine politics is a struggle among four segments of the Philippine bourgeoisie for control over the administrative and coercive organizations of the state. In this struggle the major international actors have favored one or another of these segments, and the U.S. government has sought to maximize its influence so as to protect its geopolitical interests in the region.

And so an initial, very general definition of the state in the Philippines would include several attributes. The state is, primarily, a set of coercive and administrative organizations. The state is a class state, defending the interests of the bourgeoisie as a whole; however, the state is relatively autonomous in the sense that it can take and has taken strong action detrimental to certain segments of the bourgeoisie. Recent Philippine politics can be conceptualized as a struggle among four class segments for control of the coercive and administrative organizations of the state in their attempt to implement distinctive development policies. Finally, international actors have penetrated the Philippine political system and exercise their influence to support those development and security policies which most favor them.

CLASS SEGMENTS AND THEIR ECONOMIC INTERESTS

After we briefly outline the most important segments of the bourgeoisie, we can explore the impact of the Marcos regime on their economic interests. This, in turn, allows us to link the nature of the regime directly to its ultimate collapse.

Crony Capitalism

Crony capitalism involves the use of official government position to advance private economic interests, and it is the Philippine counterpart to what is known throughout Southeast Asia as bureaucrat capitalism.[8] In most countries of the region being a high-ranking official in the military or civilian bureaucracy opens tremendous opportunities for joint-venture participation or more direct economic pay-offs. What distinguished the Philippine variant under Marcos was that most of the cronies were not government officials; certainly the most spectacular and most publicized cases involved private citizens. A crony was defined by his close personal friendship with the president or first lady and the government favoritism consequently received. In the agricultural export industries we have highlighted the activities of four presidential cronies—Eduardo Cojuangco, Jr., Roberto Benedicto, Antonio Floirendo, and Juan Ponce Enrile—and of this group only Enrile was a government official.

The cronies seem to merit being considered as a distinct class segment, because they collectively shared, in the words of Zeitlin, Neuman, and Ratcliff, "a relatively distinct position in the social process of production and, consequently, its own specific political economic requirements." The position they occupied in the social process of production was right next to the First Family's. They all served as important officials in the president's ruling political party. Their specific political-economic requirements included the maintenance of a capitalist, class-divided economy but also, and even more important, the continuation in office of President Ferdinand Marcos. The loss of office by President Marcos under conditions where the cronies could not influence his successor has meant the end of their economic empires—at least in the Philippines.[9] Benedicto, Cojuangco, and Floirendo all fled with Marcos in February 1986. They now live abroad on wealth they were able to remove from the country. Only Enrile who, along with Deputy Chief of Staff of the Armed Forces Fidel Ramos, precipitated the massive military defection from Marcos was able to make the transition to a position of power in the new government of Corazon Aquino.

State Capitalism

Throughout the world, but especially in the industrializing countries of the Third World, the importance of state enterprises in the economy has been growing. There are several reasons for this growth. The desire for development has often exceeded the capacity of a small and economically weak bourgeoisie. The channeling of billions of dollars of development aid and loans through government institutions has fostered the growth of a financial and managerial elite in these governments. That elite feels qualified to lead the effort for industrialization without necessarily depending on the private sector—a private sector whose motivation may be less a matter of national development than of private gain. The increasing need for powerful actors able to counterbalance the power and influence of the foreign investor has often required the state to take a more active role in the economy.

The Philippine state, like its counterparts elsewhere in the Third World, has gradually taken control of several important sectors of the economy. Since the declaration of martial law the state has taken ownership of Philippine Airlines; several multinational oil companies have sold all or part of their interests to the state-owned Philippine National Oil Company; and the military took over several privately held steel mills to create the National Steel Corporation. In a second pattern of state capitalism the state's financial institutions—largely the Philiippine National Bank and the Development Bank of the Philippines—have funneled capital into important companies that have suffered from the volatility of the Philippine market place, where the slightest increase in interest rates or decline in the growth rate may mean collapse of the company. Among the companies receiving such assistance have been the Marinduque Mining and Industrial Corporation and the Paper Industries Corporation of the Philippines. In both cases the corporations remained, at least temporarily, in the hands of private management, but the role of state managers increased substantially. A third pattern involves the collapse of the crony empires. The state's investment in such corporations has often been so great that when the companies finally fail (whether because of poor management, overexpansion, or a changing international market), the state has little choice but to step in and take over management in an effort to salvage something from the wreckage.

All three factors have helped the public sector grow in size and economic importance. At the end of 1981 President Marcos announced there were ninety-two parent government corporations in the Philippines and one hundred twenty subsidiaries. This total does not, for the most part, include takeovers of financially distressed corporations from the private sector. The government now owns numerous banks, finance corporations, hotels, and mines, several mills for the production of paper, textiles, and sugar, as well as construction companies, shipping lines, and steel mills. With the flight of Marcos and his cronies, the Aquino government has set up the Presidential Commission on Good Government, which has once again increased, at least temporarily, the size of government holdings in the economy. The commission has done so because it has sought to recover for the government all of the private-sector holdings acquired as ill-gotten gains of political corruption under Marcos.

In control of the state-owned corporations are technocrats and professional managers. One of the lessons that many of these professionals learned from the Marcos years is that national interests are not synonymous with the interests of private business or of any one politician. As a consequence government managers, in spite of a new emphasis on reprivatization, are likely to be vigorous in defending the role of government ownership to ensure that the benefits of industrialization accrue to the nation while at the same time they attract the maximum possible amount of new private investment, both foreign and domestic.

Production for the Local Market

In the reconstruction years after World War II imports of consumer goods, partly financed by aid, mushroomed. The matter was naturally a concern of policy makers responsible for maintaining a positive balance of trade. Robert Baldwin tells us that "in 1947 consumption goods made up 68 percent of all imports. . . . Most Philippine leaders believed that the country needed both additional export-oriented and import-replacing production in order to meet the adjustment problems associated with the gradual phasing out of reciprocal preferential relations with the U.S."[10]

In response to the high consumer goods content of total imports the country adopted import controls early in 1949. To respond to the rapid depletion of the nation's foreign currency reserves, the Philippines adopted (with the permission of the U.S. president) exchange controls that same year. The controls were effective in providing a high degree of protection for the manufacture of consumer goods. What began as an emergency tactic in balance-of-payments policy became the principal policy instrument for promoting industrialization over the 1950s.

Previously foreign manufacturers had had no incentive to invest in any sector except the processing of bulky primary products. Now the overwhelming response of U.S. manufacturers was to invest. Because the shortage of dollars limited U.S. exports to Manila, as Marcos himself would later note, "substantial American investments came into the Philippines, mainly for import substituting domestic market oriented industries. This influx was due largely to their decision to get within [Philippine] tariff walls in order to avoid being left out of a lucrative domestic market."[11]

During the 1950s it became increasingly difficult to get allocations of foreign currency to import consumer goods. Among the hard-to-import goods were "shoes, toys, pencils, automotive storage batteries, ready-mixed paints, cotton and synthetic knitted fabrics, and all made-up garments of cotton and rayon."[12]

Quite naturally these government policies had a major impact on manufacturers for the domestic market. To quote Baldwin again, "the major beneficiaries of the government's development policies have been those who own or control business in the industrial sector."[13] This Philippine entrepreneurial group also benefited from the gradual nationalization of import trade and domestic retail trade during the 1950s. The change transferred much of the domestic and international commercial sector from the hands of foreign investors and the Chinese minority to the hands of Filipinos. Filipino-owned firms could also avail themselves of subsidized credit and in many cases had preferential access to foreign exchange.

In combination these policies created an entrepreneurial group, largely but not exclusively Filipino, which depended on government protection for its continued economic well-being. In a confidential analysis of the Philippines written in 1980, the World Bank argued that the economic situation before martial law was characterized by "heavily protected and inefficient manufacturing industries, controlled by politically well-connected ethnic Filipinos, which were gradually increasing in importance despite their inefficiency and the existing [sic] of some foreign competition." Later in the same report the author examined likely bases for opposition to the Philippine government's World Bank–supported economic program. While the local industrial sector's "opposition to further eliminations of protectionism is certainly expectable, local industrialists' capacity to oppose effectively has been eroded by their own economic decline due to the concentration of economic power in the hands of the state, multinationals and Marcos' inner circle."[14]

The World Bank's record of support for export-oriented industrialization in the Third World makes it no surprise that the Philippine government, on the advice of the Bank, took steps since the

1960s which significantly weakened the import-substitution industrialists. Among the most important of these steps have been devaluations of the peso, decontrol of the economy, reductions in the
wage rates of the working class and other low-income consumers,
an increase in subsidies for export-oriented business, and a reduction in tariff protection for domestic manufacturers.[15]

In this attack on the ISI bourgeoisie the state has been supported
by the technical expertise and political power of the World Bank
and the International Monetary Fund. The concrete political-economic requirements of the import-substituting segment of the
bourgeoisie have been consistently eroded over the last two decades. Producers for the domestic market have responded in various ways. Some entrepreneurs shifted capital into export industries; others left the country, taking their capital with them. Many
producers for the local market who are Filipino have become more
nationalistic and more politicized, as the World Bank predicted in
1980. These members of the elite occupy a difficult position, and
they often vacillated in the intensity and direction of their political
participation. They consistently opposed the crony capitalists, became increasingly anti-Marcos, and played an important role in his
final downfall. They are nationalistic but fear too close an association with leftists, who may be not just nationalist but also anti-
capitalist. Their numbers are small, and their political power has
weakened with the collapse of the Philippine economy. As a group,
however, they will play a pivotal role in any post-Marcos regime,
and they may be especially important in determining the shape of
the working relationship that emerges between the Aquino government and the International Monetary Fund.

Production for the International Market

Martial law, its attendant policy changes, and the foreign investment it attracted were all a boon to the export of manufactures by
the Philippines. In the ten years between 1971 and 1980 exports of
electrical and electronic equipment and components jumped from
$280,000 to $671 million. Garment exports increased from $36
million to $500 million. The export of handicrafts grew in value
from $9 million to $154 million. Other commodities showing sharp
increases in the dollar value of exports during the decade included

food products and beverages, chemicals, furniture, footwear, toys, and sporting goods.[16]

These exports rose because of significant new investment during the 1970s in the manufacturing sector. This investment was stimulated by policy changes begun in the 1960s and fully implemented after the declaration of martial law. The power and wages of the working class were sharply curtailed through strict surveillance of the unions and restrictions on the right to strike. Nationalist legislation and decisions by the Supreme Court which threatened the security or profitability of foreign investment were reversed under martial law. Since the end of World War II Congress had refused to negotiate a new treaty governing relations with Japan, but with the demise of Congress, Marcos quickly signed a new executive agreement with Japan which, in turn, led to an upsurge in Japanese investments in the Philippines. In all these initiatives, support from the U.S. government, the World Bank, and the International Monetary Fund, both as intellectual justification and as economic aid, gave Marcos and his technocrats the tools to see initiatives through to implemented policies.

Broadly speaking, the commercial, labor, and investment policies that the Philippines was being encouraged to adopt were welcomed by two categories of exporters—exporters of manufactured products, and exporters of raw materials both agricultural and mineral. These two sectors of the export economy were deeply integrated into the world economy and were characterized by mixed patterns of ownership—much foreign direct investment but also a number of joint ventures, as well as locally owned enterprises producing under contract for multinational corporations. It was from these two sectors of the export economy that local allies of the World Bank and International Monetary Fund emerged. These allies supported the shift away from import-substitution industrialization and favored the lowering of tariffs, barriers to foreign investment, and wages. Internally, the group differed over location of infrastructure investment and other government incentives to private initiative. As the agricultural export sector fell increasingly under the control of presidential cronies, the transparent use of presidential power to favor certain individuals and sectors of the economy destroyed the sense of community and common interest within the export sector.

THE INTERNATIONAL CONTEXT
OF PHILIPPINE POLITICS

For the Philippine state, the overriding factor in the international context during the twentieth century has been its relations with the United States.[17] Dominant segments of the bourgeoisie have been able to extract not only resources from the domestic Philippine economy but also a variety of resources—legitimacy, economic aid, military assistance, prestige, and ideological support—from the United States.

Until the 1950s agricultural exporters were clearly the dominant segment of the Philippine bourgeoisie. They depended on favored access to the lucrative U.S. market for the profitability of their exports. The United States also provided intellectual legitimacy for an anticommunist foreign policy and for a development model based on the principle of comparative advantage.

Throughout the 1950s and part of the 1960s the import-substituting bourgeoisie was dominant in the Philippines, building much of its strength on an appeal to nationalism. However, this segment of the bourgeoisie was by no means completely Filipino. Large parts of the ISI sector were under the ownership or control of foreign investors. The policy environment, through its provision of state support for investment in manufacturing for the local market, was supportive of expansion by U.S. and other multinational corporations at a time when the multinationals themselves were seeking outlets abroad.[18] Also, even though the controls that the Philippine government had placed on imports and the convertibility of foreign exchange ran counter to liberal economic doctrine, the United States acquiesced to Philippine support of import-substitution industrialization. Similarly America acquiesced to protection of domestic manufacturing by Europe and Japan. It was part of the cost the United States chose to pay in order to maintain both its own hegemony and the stability of the liberal world economy.[19]

In the late 1960s, and especially after the declaration of martial law, the United States joined the International Monetary Fund and the World Bank to support a reopening of the Philippine economy. Their support has furthered the regnant development model—export-oriented development—and has been based on a shift in the international division of labor. The Philippines was to become another export platform for low-wage manufactured goods to be sold worldwide. Ideological and intellectual support for this effort came primarily from the World Bank.[20] The United States also provided military and economic assistance to strengthen the state. And so the United States served as a handmaiden in the assumption of power, through the declaration of martial law, of that segment of the bourgeoisie most closely linked to the export-oriented model of development.

This strengthening of the Philippine state, through increased international assistance and the use of martial law powers to quell domestic opposition, was important for the technocrats within the state elite. It increased their insulation from the demands of civil society, allowing them to speak for the interests of international donors and those segments of the bourgeoisie both foreign and local which were interested in manufacturing for export. Insulated though the technocrats may have been from civil society, however, what the case studies show is that they had no power to resist the demands of Marcos and his cronies.

So high was the level of political interference and mismanagement of the economy that it raises an obvious question: Why did the international community choose to lend its legitimacy and capital to the Marcos government? Why did the World Bank designate the Philippines a "country of concentration" to which Bank assistance would be "higher than average for countries of similar size and income?"[21] One answer is that the international community thought it could convince the Marcos government to pay the political costs necessary to implement fully the export-oriented model of development. This confidence must have been bolstered by the high profile of and seemingly important role played by technocrats in the Philippine government. If the technocrats were to prevail in their internal struggles, they needed the fullest possible backing, both ideologically and with additional capital to overcome domestic political opposition.[22]

Another explanation for continued external support for the Marcos government rests on the strategic importance of the Philippines. The major U.S. military bases in the country were important staging areas during the Indochina War. Since the end of that war, though, the bases seem to have become even more important.[23]

One analyst has suggested that the United States has at least four military objectives in the western Pacific.

> First, to support US bilateral and multilateral defense commitments with countries in Southeast and Northeast Asia, Australia, and New Zealand. Second, to protect the sea lines of communication and trade routes which press through the strategic waterways of Southeast Asia that are of major importance to the US and Japan. Third, to support the American presence in the Indian Ocean and Persian Gulf region, particularly Diego Garcia. Fourth, to counter the increasing Soviet military presence in Southeast Asia.[24]

Those who agree with this statement of U.S. military objectives in the region usually go on to argue that the military bases in the Philippines are the most effective, the most convenient, and the cheapest way of meeting the objectives.[25]

After the fall of South Vietnam one pressing foreign policy requirement for Gerald Ford's administration was to show that the United States intended to remain a power in the western Pacific. President Ford visited Asia to reaffirm the nation's will and commitment to the region, and during this Asian visit, in December 1975, Gerald Ford and Ferdinand Marcos issued a joint communiqué in which they

> considered that the treaty of August 30, 1951 [Mutual Defense Treaty between the Republic of the Philippines and the United States of America] enhanced the defense of both countries, strengthened the security of the Pacific region, and contributed to the maintenance of world peace. They agreed that the military bases used by the US in the Philippines remain important in maintaining an effective United States presence in the Western Pacific in support of these mutual objectives.[26]

Even Jimmy Carter, who placed marginally greater emphasis on concern for the protection of human rights in the Philippines, sent Walter Mondale to Manila in May 1978. The visit forcefully demonstrated to the Filipino public, through print and broadcast media completely controlled by the government, that Marcos still had the backing of Washington.

It was also under President Carter that a five-year agreement was negotiated to amend the original 1947 Military Bases Agreement. In lobbying to get the agreement's compensation package through the U.S. Congress, Carter argued that the base facilities in the Philippines have an "importance which is not limited to the western Pacific but which extends . . . to much wider areas of the Indian Ocean and entire Middle East." He went on to say that "recent events in Southeast Asia, the Indian Ocean and the Middle East have raised doubts about the willingness of the United States to sustain support for its friends and to honor its obligations. I am determined to dispel such unwarranted doubts."[27] As part of the 1979 agreement the United States contributed to the Philippines, over a five-year period, $50 million for military assistance, $250 million for foreign military sales credits, and $200 million for security supporting assistance. While the overall security assistance program for East Asia was declining, assistance to the Philippines was increasing.

With the election of Ronald Reagan, public (and probably private) expressions of concern about human rights violations in the Philippines declined. In its first few years the Reagan administration warmly embraced President Marcos. In June 1981 Secretary of State Alexander Haig traveled to Manila, and that same month Vice-President George Bush was in Manila representing the United States at the inauguration of Marcos after his reelection as president (against only token opposition). In April 1982 Secretary of Defense Caspar Weinberger was in the Philippines and toured both Clark Air Base and Subic Naval Base.

These visits were capped by Marcos's visit to Washington in September 1982. His reception in the White House by Reagan, reported on every Philippine television station and in daily front-page stories in the newspapers, banished any remaining doubts about the strength of his U.S. support. The stream of high-level visitors to Manila, plus the Marcos visit to the United States, established a record of public support perhaps unequaled anywhere else.

This American support for Marcos and reaffirmations of the importance of American bases in the Philippines have in large part reflected growing concern in Washington over Soviet access to Vietnamese military facilities, across the South China Sea, and the increased need for a "back-door route" to the Indian Ocean and the Middle East. But it merely continued patterns of relations established earlier. The United States provided the Philippines between 1946 and 1983 with a total of $2.4044 billion in economic assistance ($676.6 million in loans and $1.728 billion in grants) and $1.2071 billion in military assistance ($294.1 million in loans and $913 million in grants).[28] In addition, slightly more than three thousand members of the Armed Forces of the Philippines received advanced military training in the United States between 1970 and 1979.[29] This U.S.-trained and equipped military was instrumental in both the centralization of state power and the consolidation of control by Ferdinand Marcos. The strengthening of the Philippine military went hand-in-hand with a favorable climate for the geopolitical interests of the United States in the region.[30]

Several factors have thus combined to produce massive international support, support that sustained and prolonged the Marcos regime. The Philippines has a tremendous importance for U.S. national defense planners. The World Bank and the IMF thought that in Marcos they had a modern authoritarian who was going to insulate his technocrats and give them a free hand. As domestic political opposition to the World Bank model of export-oriented industrialization was inevitable, the international donor community was determined to provide the ideological backing and capital needed to support the technocrats and their allies in the export segment of the bourgeoisie. In addition there was a close personal friendship between Ferdinand Marcos and Ronald Reagan. In this friendship Marcos was viewed as an old ally of the United States who was struggling with a growing, Marxist-led rural insurgency. Many observers felt that he needed and deserved U.S. support. Taken together these conditions resulted not just in continued but in sharply increased international support for a highly unsavory government.

IMPLICATIONS OF THE PHILIPPINE CASE

If the Philippines is to be placed in theoretical and comparative perspectives, then, as I suggested in Chapter 1, we have to address two sets of concerns. First, in Stephan Haggard's words, we need to know "what domestic political factors account for the different development trajectories of the East Asian and Latin American NICs." Second and "equally important in explaining specific policy reforms is the political independence of state elites from societal actors." The historical and case studies of the preceding chapters focus our attention on the Philippines both as an individual case and as part of larger, comparative patterns of development in the Third World. I emphasize eight specific findings here. Some re-state or refine positions taken earlier by other scholars of Third World development; some are unique to the Philippine case.

First, and most important, to differentiate the Philippines from other developing nations it is necessary, in the words of Fernando Henrique Cardoso and Enzo Faletto, "to consider in their totality the 'historic specificities,' both economic and social, underlying the developmental processes at the national and international levels. . . . It is necessary to analyze how the underdeveloped economies were linked historically to the world market and how internal social groups defined the outward-directed relations implicit in underdevelopment."[31] Cardoso and Faletto thus direct our attention to the historical specificities that determine the nature of the linkage between a Third World economy and the world market.[32] In the Philippines the linkage began in the colonial era as an almost perfect example of classic dependence. The country was an exporter of raw materials and an importer of manufactures. It was incorporated into patterns of trade dictated by and shaped to the interests of the colonizer and the domestic elite. This domestic elite, for most of Philippine history, found that it could maximize its own interests by collaborating with the colonizer, not by joining with dominated groups and classes in a concerted challenge to the colonizer.

Yet out of this classic dependence, and contrary to the predictions of some early proponents of dependency analysis, emerged growth and economic diversification. The international economy—because of wars, depressions, and changes in the international division of labor—encouraged first, the processing of bulky materials in the Third World, and later, investment in manufacturing. Domestically the growth of entrepreneurial skills and economic opportunities led to a gradual diversification of the economy and the class structure. This diversification appears to have been more tentative and gradual in the Philippines than in other nations with similar resource endowments and opportunities for change.

The reasons for this difference in the Philippine experience lead to the next finding.

Second, in accounting for different development trajectories we must look not just at the impact of the international economy but, as Haggard suggests, also at domestic political factors. Philippine domestic politics, as we have seen, has been important. That the early Philippine economic elite was based in the agroexport sector, and that this economic elite was also dominant politically, meant little domestic incentive or interest in the industrialization of the country. It was only the economic crisis immediately after World War II which provoked even the limited industrialization of import substitution. And this observation leads to another finding.

Third, the sequence and timing of industrialization is of utmost significance. The historic specificity of Philippine import substitution is that ISI occurred at a time when, and in an international environment where foreign investors dominated the ISI sector. Elsewhere the ISI sector arose from the crisis of world depression (Latin America) or the decisions of a colonial master (Taiwan and South Korea). In such cases the timing and international environment were different and resulted in a larger role for domestic entrepreneurs and an earlier escape from the confines of the colonial economy. For the Philippines, the parity amendment and the fact that ISI occurred at a time when U.S. manufacturers were ready and willing to expand abroad combined to guarantee that control of the ISI sector of the Philippine economy would be in relative terms more foreign than domestic.

Fourth, to explain specific policy reforms we must turn, in Haggard's words, to the "political independence of state elites from societal actors." This independence is, of course, a product of many factors. In the Philippine case the nature of colonial rule and the lateness of ISI have been important. By way of contrast is the case of Brazil where, Peter Evans tells us, a triple alliance of state, local, and multinational capital developed during the 1960s. The autonomy of the Brazilian state was a product not just of its military government but rather of the control of productive resources. Of the early years after the military coup of 1964, Evans says that,

> given the central place in the process of accumulation that state enterprises had carved out for themselves, it would have been extremely disruptive to try to dislodge them, but the military also had positive

reasons for supporting state enterprises. To abolish them would have meant diminished control over the economy, which would have run directly counter to the government's strategy. Despite the pro-laissez-faire convictions of many of the military's early supporters, the major impact of the military's takeover was a centralization of economic power.[33]

The Philippines, too, developed state enterprises, among them infant manufacturing industries and other capital-intensive pre-requisites such as electric power generation for private-sector industrialization. Yet in the Philippines it was not a military elite that directed industrialization during the 1960s. Rather, the election of Diosdado Macapagal to the presidency in 1962 and his reopening of the Philippine economy under the guidance of the IMF signaled the dismantling of the state's role in direct economic production. It was at this point that foreign investment in the Philippine economy increased and, as Chapter 4 outlined, the increase was especially significant for the fruit products industry. The state chose not to take an active role in these enterprises; rather, it served as a passive provider of land for foreign enterprise. The state elite was not independent, nor were the dominant groups in the Philippines of the 1960s military modernizers interested in centralized control. They were civilian politicians, politicians most responsive to agro-exporters and foreign investors. They reflected years of colonial tutelage from the Americans in the basics of the liberal international economic order—free trade and the free flow of capital. And so Macapagal and his advisers pledged a laissez-faire economy with a very limited role for the government. Government policy stimulated new investment and a growth in agricultural exports. It also resulted in a slowdown in industrialization. The average annual growth rate in manufacturing value added was 9.2 percent in the period 1956–62, dropped off to 8.5 percent in 1962–68, and fell further, to 5.4 percent, between 1968 and 1973.[34]

At the end of the 1960s and in the early 1970s the Philippines had no clear direction to its development policies. Whatever policy incentives existed had developed out of the tumult of electoral politics and the linkage of the Philippines to the international market. The Philippines did not respond quickly or adequately to the growing international demand for such low-wage manufactures as textiles and shoes and computer chips. Yet during the latter sixties and into the seventies international advisers were encouraging the Philippines to begin the transition to a new model of export-oriented industrialization which had served other East Asian nations and the city-states of Hong Kong and Singapore so well.

In short, the international economy and the international division of labor had shifted, leaving the Philippines behind. Despite the commodity boom of 1973–74, the long-term trend in the international economy was away from commodities and toward higher demand for manufactures. But domestic political factors prevented the Philippines from achieving the transition to export-oriented industrialization—that transition could not occur until after the declaration of martial law. At this point the state became the single most important actor in the Philippine political economy.

Fifth, the larger the political sphere at the end of the "easy phase" of ISI, the case of the Philippines suggests, the more difficult will be the transition to the new models of development based on low-wage manufacturing or further and more capital-intensive import substitution. The work of Guillermo O'Donnell is instructive, because in 1972 the Philippine class structure and political sphere were similar to those of several Latin American nations.[35] A large, politically active labor force, a powerful group of import-substituting industrialists (many of whom were foreign investors), political parties, and a relatively more institutionalized political system based on elite democracy—all these factors made the transition difficult in Latin America and in the Philippines. In South Korea and Taiwan, by contrast, the political sphere never expanded during ISI and so did not have to contract dramatically to accommodate the changes necessary for a transition to export-oriented development. Timing was again very important. Although I have not sought to document the difficulties involved in replicating the East Asian model of export-oriented development, it is easy in this age of growing protectionism and dramatic technical improvements in the field of labor-saving machinery to see the disadvantages inherent in being a decade behind the pioneers in the model. The disadvantages and difficulties of moving to an export-oriented version of development make it no surprise that the Philippines and other late industrializers have needed a strong state.

Sixth, the Philippine case shows the necessity of clearly differentiating between the state and regime, for the strong state in the Philippines must be distinguished in important features from the strong states of the more successful NICs.[36] The dynamics of the international economy—expressed primarily through the actions of a finite number of international actors (multinational corporations, the IMF and the World Bank, and the aid donor governments)—have reinforced the state in the Philippines. That process began before Ferdinand Marcos assumed office, and the state is likely to be an important actor now that Marcos has passed from the scene.

No doubt the support for the Philippine state which came from international actors was designed to streamline the state, to make it a more efficient administrator of the process of economic development. Support for the military was consonant with America's strategic interests and needed to combat internal opposition to continued class rule. Since Ferdinand Marcos was first elected in 1965, however, international support for the Philippine state has had to be coursed through his regime. Most international actors believed that their interests were very similar to those of the Marcos regime. Marcos was, throughout his twenty years in office, a firm supporter of a more thoroughgoing opening of the Philippine economy and a larger role for foreign investors. At the Seventh Annual Philippine Business Conference held in 1981, for example, both the president and his prime minister, Cesar Virata, promised to reduce the number of state-owned and controlled corporations. They also emphasized a traditional view of the government in which government sets objectives, lays down rules, provides infrastructure support, and then leaves business to private entrepreneurs.[37] Similarly for agriculture, in 1979 Minister Arturo Tanco told the American Chamber of Commerce in the Philippines that "what you have done in sugar, coconut products, rubber and others, you can do in other agribusiness areas." He assured his audience that agribusiness ventures "are desired" and "will be rewarded" by the government.[38]

Ferdinand Marcos, unlike the international actors who supported the Philippine state, was always clear that his interests were not completely synonymous with those of the multinationals, or the U.S. government, or the World Bank/IMF group. His primary goal was to remain in office. In declining health, beset by grievous national economic problems, and under constant attack from internal and external sources, he clung tenaciously to the presidency. He continued until his very last day in office to use international support for the state to maintain his hold on the Philippine political system. As long as Marcos remained president, he was able to use the coercive and administrative organizations of the state to his own end. He threatened, bluffed, and took action whenever possible to see that, while he followed the prescribed path to development, while he enlarged the role that foreign investors could play, he did nothing to endanger his own continued rule.

We can illustrate the importance of the distinction between state and regime concretely and starkly. The fall of Marcos and the assumption of the presidency by Corazon Aquino, it can be argued, represents a change of regime; but at the same time the basic pact of domination in the Philippines has not changed dramatically, and the Aquino government is a continuation of essentially the same coalition of dominant class segments and of the same pattern of class domination. This statement obviously requires elaboration and clarification, and I return to it below, but part of the reason for this conclusion I can state here: the Philippines remains enmeshed both in security relations with the United States and in economic relations with powerful economic actors.

Seventh, in the case of many Third World nations, and certainly in the case of the Philippines, we should conceive of the basic pact of domination in transnational terms. The security interests of the U.S. military are of particular importance in, for example, South Korea, Taiwan, Pakistan, Egypt, and the Philippines. The provision of military assistance, rent for bases (in the Philippines, $900 million for the period 1984–89), and military advisory groups to these countries insures that at the level of the state, security interests are defined more in international terms than in terms of the national security of the individual Third World country.

Countries such as the Philippines also have a long history of cooperation with the World Bank and the International Monetary Fund. Major agreements between the International Monetary Fund and the Philippine government have come in 1962, 1970, 1976, 1979, and 1985. In each agreement the Philippines has given up a certain measure of national sovereignty over exchange rates, money supply, inflation, taxes, trade policy, foreign investment policy, and industrial policy in exchange for economic assistance.[39]

Obviously the U.S. Pentagon, the World Bank, and the International Monetary Fund are not class segments, and so they do not fit well with the idea of the state being at the highest level a pact of domination among segments of the bourgeoisie. These transnational actors do, however, defend a liberal international order, an international order built on free trade, the free flow of investment, the sanctity of private property, and limited governments. Therefore they tend to defend and enhance the international role of the multinational corporations, and the corporations and their owners do constitute a class segment and an important element in the pact of domination.

Eighth, the tendency of much analysis to concentrate on the level of the state, to remain at a high level of abstraction, underestimates the importance of the regime. As Cardoso says, "the character of the state—i.e., the structure of class domination and the economic system upon which this structure rests—imposes some limits on the form of the political regime." But within those limits he also emphasizes that "the capacity for control varies among different authoritarian regimes due to multiple factors." Those factors include the circumstances under which the regimes come to power, the degree of weakness or strength of civil society, technical factors such as the efficiency of the repressive apparatus, and finally, whether or not the authoritarian regime has an effective political party through which it can rule.[40]

What Cardoso is suggesting and what, I think, the Philippine case shows is that, despite certain similarities among the various NICs at the level of the state, we need to look at the particularities of the regime that is in power. In the Philippines an analysis that considered just the level of the state, or just the level of the regime, would be incomplete. We can appreciate the importance of this point by once again turning to the collapse of the Marcos regime and the rise of the Aquino regime.

THE COLLAPSE OF THE MARCOS REGIME

The movement under Marcos toward a more open economy based on export-oriented manufacturing, brought about largely at the urging of international supporters of the Philippine state, exacerbated the inequalities of the underlying agroexport economy. Despite some growth of manufactured exports, the Philippines was unable to generate sufficient employment to accomplish the gradual improvement of wage rates and living standards (as well as a lowering of economic inequality) which observers have identified with export-oriented industrialization in South Korea and Taiwan. Numerous factors contributed. Population growth rates have diminished markedly, but even so, approximately 700,000 new job seekers were added to the labor market every year for much of the 1970s and 1980s. Land reform in the Philippines has not been as thoroughgoing as in South Korea and Taiwan, and as a consequence rural employment opportunities have been more limited. This, in turn, contributed to an influx of rural workers into the cities. Finally, because the pattern of political control I have documented for the rural sector is also evident in large parts of the urban economy, the Philippines failed to attract as much new investment and reinvestment as did the more successful newly industrializing countries. Levels of poverty, malnutrition, and inequality have all increased over the last decade in the Philippines, and these have contributed to rising levels of political discontent.

The existence of a transnationalized, dependent, and capitalist state means that the domestic economy must be reshaped to meet the needs of the changing international division of labor. But the Philippines failed in its efforts to emulate the economic miracles of East Asia. The political reorganization brought on by martial law did, it is true, reduce the size of the political sphere. Technocrats were to a certain extent insulated from the demands of civil society. They had great success in areas where their policies did not conflict with the personal political requirements of Ferdinand Marcos. They could discipline labor and reduce wages. They could implement new policies to attract foreign investment and stimulate exports of manufactured goods. But where the technocrats failed was in their inability to implement policies that would have had real political costs for Marcos. The import-substitution industrialists could block reductions in tariffs because they were a potent political force that employed a great deal of labor. Likewise policies to rationalize the haphazard and politicized investment pattern in the processing of agroexport crops and to reinvest surplus from these industries were always blocked by presidential cronies whose extraction of surplus was vital to the maintenance of the Marcos presidency.

The unique character of the Marcos regime has obvious political implications. Under Marcos the absence of regular, legal, and effective avenues to influence government policy, or simply to vote out of office unpopular leaders, led vast numbers of Filipinos to seek other forms of political participation. Students demonstrated for educational reforms and lower tuition; workers went on strike for better wages and working conditions; opposition newspapers sprang up to compete with the government-controlled press; rallies were held to demand justice for political detainees and victims of military atrocities; peasants organized to reduce land rents and to oppose expansion at their expense by the agribusiness plantations. Each of these forms of political participation opposed the continued rule of Marcos, but at a more significant level it was political participation that tended to weaken continued class rule. This is certainly not to say that all participants in political protest in the Philippines favored revolution and transition to a classless society. Yet most recognized the fundamental, structural problems that plagued the nation. The farsighted among them knew that getting rid of Marcos would not solve the most basic of the nation's problems.

The upsurge in political participation during the 1980s had several significant effects. It provoked a crisis of legitimacy for Marcos which was even more severe than the challenge he had faced in the late 1960s and early 1970s and which led to his declaration of martial law. The assassination of his chief political opponent, Benigno Aquino, Jr., on August 21, 1983, sparked a quantum leap in opposition, because most Filipinos appeared to believe that Marcos or his military men were behind the murder. Emboldened by the greater political participation of the people, opposition political parties made a new effort to organize and prepare for elections. The politicization of the Filipino people was also partly cause and partly effect of the efforts of the National Democratic Front, the Communist Party of the Philippines, and the military wing of the party, the New People's Army. Estimates vary, but it is believed that the number of full-time, armed guerrillas fighting in the New People's Army grew dramatically in the early 1980s; and by 1985 the guerrillas numbered around fifteen thousand. The National Democratic Front, a broad coalition of cause-oriented groups encompassing peasants, workers, intellectuals, nationalists, white-collar middle-class workers, and nationalist entrepreneurs, became a potent voice in favor of nationalism, democracy, and an end to U.S. military bases in the Philippines. In the final months of the Marcos regime even parts of the bourgeoisie were talking to members of the National Democratic Front about cooperating in the effort to get rid of Marcos and about the outlines of a post-Marcos government and economy.

At the same time the upsurge in political participation led segments of the international and domestic pact of domination which makes up the Philippine state to demand reforms of the Marcos regime. Their pressure took several forms. In exchange for a new stabilization agreement with the International Monetary Fund, for example, the Marcos regime was required to reduce state intervention in the economy and, in particular, reduce the amount of favoritism shown to presidential cronies.

Growing domestic opposition to the Marcos regime led the United States to rethink its previously unqualified support for Marcos. Washington began to put pressure on Marcos to hold free and fair elections. The problem for the United States, and for other international actors with an interest in the Philippines, was how to resurrect the liberal democratic regime they thought they had had before the declaration of martial law without at the same time endangering the gains made under martial law—gains that represented considerable progress toward the creation of an open economy based on production for the international market. In the face of this dilemma, Marcos was still an important political figure. After analyzing Philippine prospects in light of massive demonstrations protesting the assassination of Aquino, the U.S. National Security Council wrote that

> reforms are likely in the short run to weaken some bases of support for the current [Marcos] government, which will resist many of them. While President Marcos at this stage is part of the problem he is also necessarily part of the solution. We need to be able to work with him and to try to influence him through a well-orchestrated policy of incentives and disincentives to set the stage for peaceful and eventual

157

transition to a successor government whenever that takes place. Marcos, for his part, will try to use us to remain in power indefinitely.[41]

Growing domestic opposition to class rule and the rule of Marcos, plus the increased international pressure, presaged the end of the Marcos regime. The demands placed on the Marcos regime by the transnational pact of domination were designed to forestall any concerted challenge to continued class domination. Reforms were called for in the military, economic, and political spheres. All this took place, moreover, in an environment of economic decline caused by slumping commodity prices, massive mismanagement and fraud, the unavailability of new short-term credit, and massive capital flight from the Philippines. Freedom of maneuver for the Marcos regime was shrinking, and the regime's capacity for control was slipping away. Marcos did not have an effective mass party that could have coopted the opposition, he had a party that was no more than a conglomeration of local political leaders who were personally loyal to him as long as they benefited by their association with him. Through the early 1980s members of this party had begun to drift away, a process that accelerated in 1985 and 1986 as the weaknesses of the regime became more apparent. The Marcos regime was also dependent on huge sums of money siphoned out of the agroexport industries. When commodity prices slumped and people stopped delivering crops to the mills, two things happened: the political machine lost a source of money, and, just as important, many planters, farmers, laborers, and tenants were driven to oppose the Marcos regime.

Not only was the Marcos regime weakening over time, but its security forces were counterproductive. The use of coercion—brutal methods of crowd control, undisciplined troops in the countryside, torture, summary execution of innocent people, massacres of villagers suspected of supporting the New People's Army, and strategic hamletting—drove more and more people to seek political change, violent political change if necessary.

In short, the reforms demanded of the Marcos regime could not have been implemented without fatally undermining the support base of the regime. At the same time the corruption, mismanagement, and violence of the regime in defense of its own private interests ultimately led to its downfall.

THE NEW REGIME AND THE ROLE
OF THE AGROEXPORT INDUSTRIES

At the level of the state, at the level of the pact of domination, the task in the mid-1980s was to defend not the Marcos regime but continued class rule. The multiple, structural problems of the Philippines, I believe, are not solely the result of the authoritarian aspirations of a political strong man and his avaricious friends and relatives. Getting rid of Marcos will solve neither the problems of the agricultural export industries nor the larger problems of the Philippines. In the absence of fundamental structural change in land ownership, patterns of political participation, and economic development the Philippine state will retain the same characteristics even after the demise of the Marcos regime. Any successor regime is bound to confront the same demands for protection of class domination, the same need for revenue to finance industrialization, and the same requirement for political mechanisms that will control the agricultural elites and the countryside. It is this insight which arises from the theoretical advances made in the study of the state. It is an insight not yet fully recognized by those who identify Marcos and other authoritarian rulers as the source of all evil. Nor is it recognized by those who conceptualize the Philippine state as a tool of either the United States or the bourgeoisie as a whole, because they fail to acknowledge the relative autonomy of the state in the Philippine context.[42]

If we consider the four class segments that, I argued earlier, constituted the pact of domination during the Marcos era—state capitalists, crony capitalists, producers for the domestic market, and producers for the international market—the only segment to have suffered immediate damage because of the fall of Marcos is that of the crony capitalists. The Philippines remains committed to an export-oriented model of development with perhaps even greater emphasis on agriculture. Overall economic guidance continues to come from the IMF; within a month of the beginning of the Aquino presidency the Fund had extended a standby credit facility of 615 million special drawing rights (worth U.S. $710.8 million) under an agreement that according to one observer gives the Fund "considerable say over the country's economic policies. The country must submit to quarterly comparisons of its economic performance against key targets. Favourable findings by IMF teams are required for drawdowns against the facility. The drawdowns also serve as triggers for separate credit releases from the country's 483 bank-creditors."[43]

Slightly higher wages, more economic opportunities, and a more progressive taxation system may produce some relative redistribution of wealth under the Aquino government. The new government did not come to power at the forefront of a new class coalition, however, and it is not a revolutionary government in that sense. The position of the landed elite is apparently safe. President Aquino is reported to have said in June 1986 that "only idle lands of the government will be included in the land reform program, and lands that are productive will not be touched." She also said that she is "not inclined to include sugarlands under land reform as studies show that the peculiarity of sugar production is such that it would not be economically feasible to cut up such lands into small parcels."[44]

Sugar trading is to be privatized, and the old monopoly structure has been replaced with a new and simplified sugar regulatory administration. This new administration is not likely to challenge the highly unequal and hierarchical relations of production within the industry. The administration is made up of one representative each of the government, the planters, and the millers. Not represented are small farmers, tenants, and workers in the industry. The private sector has already sent a mission to Washington and hopes, as the sugar industry has hoped for at least fifty years, to increase its quota in the protected and lucrative U.S. market.[45] At the time of the mission the U.S. price was 22 cents per pound, almost three times the world price of 8 cents a pound.

In the long run the state capitalists may also find their role somewhat diminished. In 1986 the World Bank offered two loans totaling U.S. $300 million for the privatization of some government corporations—one will be aimed at the public corporate sector and the other, from the International Finance Corporation, at privatization of government holdings in banks acquired from the private sector. The objective is to "transfer government acquired properties such as cement plants, textile mills, mining firms and others to private business."[46] This reprivatization is planned to take some time and may never be completely implemented. In 1984, it has been estimated, the government owned or controlled corporations that had total assets of 691 billion pesos (at a time when twenty pesos bought one dollar), and to this total the Philippine Commission on Good Government—newly created under Aquino—has added considerably. In the first ten weeks of its existence, according to one report, the commission sequestered the documents, assets, or shares of stock of 180 corporations, the assets of just 46 of which totaled another 52 billion pesos.[47]

The import-substituting segment of the bourgeoisie seems to have its defenders within the new regime. Minister of Trade and Industry José Concepcion, Jr., has said that "the government will continue to resist all pressures to totally remove controls on imports because most industries are having extreme difficulties." "A delayed and staggered implementation of the import liberalization program is one of the several measures the MTI [Ministry of Trade and Industry] has taken to encourage investments," he said, "noting that it would help shield existing and prospective operations from undue competition from imports."[48]

This suggests that at the level of the state the group to have benefited most from the transition to the Aquino government has been producers for the international market, and they will continue to benefit. These producers for the international market will be fully supported by international actors such as the World Bank, the International Monetary Fund, and the U.S. government. The Aquino government has successfully consolidated and strengthened class rule.

Crony capitalists have been eliminated from the pact of domination. State power has been used against the crony capitalists, in part to solidify the continued rule of the rest of the bourgeoisie. Likewise, the role of the state capitalists is now likely to diminish in the face of continued hostility from creditors and the commitment of the Aquino government to avoid the excesses of its predecessor.

The import-substituting segment of the bourgeoisie will continue to decline in political power in the face of continued pressure from the World Bank and the International Monetary Fund. The Aquino government will attempt to protect this segment, which will be a source of friction between the government and its international creditors. The real winners in the recent political drama of the Philippines have thus been exporters, prime among them the agroexporters.

Corazon Aquino's government is a vast improvement over that of Marcos in many ways—obvious examples are her respect for human rights, the move toward democratization, the attempt to recover the ill-gotten gains of the Marcos era, and the new spirit of optimism she has brought to the nation. All are noteworthy achievements. If the level of analysis for our study of political economy were to remain the regime, then it might be appropriate to conclude that the transition from Marcos to Aquino was sufficient to eliminate most of the social, political, and economic evils of the period of authoritarian rule. In retrospect we might even conclude that Marcos had accomplished something positive through his destruction of the power of the agroexport elite in the countryside.

But, as I have argued throughout this book, political economy must be concerned with two levels of analysis, the regime and the state. The problems of the agricultural export industries are not limited to those brought about by the political manipulation of Marcos. The agricultural industries generate extreme inequality as well as high levels of malnutrition and poverty, and so they contribute to growing class conflict in the countryside. These agricultural industries are, in turn, symptomatic of larger problems in the Philippine economy.

The change in regimes has had little impact at the level of the state. The pattern of class domination, while no longer so harshly repressive, remains relatively unchanged. There is little prospect for change in land ownership. The Philippines remains dependent on agriculture for the bulk of its export earnings—indeed, new foreign investment is being asked to participate in the further expansion of the agribusiness sector of the economy.

Elimination of the Marcos cronies, coupled with the announced plans of the Aquino government to break up monopolies in sugar and coconut trading, invite in new foreign investment, and reinvigorate the agricultural export sector of the economy, will most likely have two effects. First, they will restore the strength of the agricultural elite. Second, they will resolidify the transnational pact of domination. The coercive and administrative powers of the state will once again be used to defend the interests of agroexporters.

For the study of comparative political and economic development, the Philippine case is suggestive. At the level of the state we have seen how factors as diverse as Spanish and American colonial policy, U.S. military interests, the political strength at the local level of the landed elite, and the influential role played by the International Monetary Fund and the World Bank have combined to create a transnational pact of domination. These diverse actors all share an interest in continued class rule, continued freedom for the flow of capital into and out of the country, continued incentives for investment in agricultural exports, and a continued role for the Philippines as a forward-basing area for U.S. military forces.

If we are to understand the political economy of the Philippines, therefore, and most probably of other Third World nations as well, we cannot look at internal domestic factors alone. In the early 1970s Marcos was able to embark on a new path to development only with the full support of the international segment of the bourgeois pact of domination. Without this support he would not have been able to use the extensive powers of the state for the transition to export-led industrialization—and for his own private political ends.

In addition to showing the importance of the state as a unit of analysis, the Philippine case also validates Stephan Haggard's argument that domestic political factors help account for different development trajectories. The international economic environment, I would argue, has been instrumental in shaping the broad outlines of most Third World development trajectories. In the case of the Philippines, however, as we have seen, these international forces are mediated through local actors. Ferdinand Marcos as president was at the focal point of international and domestic forces all of which had an impact on the country's development trajectory. It was his political style, his greed, his insistence on centralized, personal control, and his interaction with other important local political actors which determined the Philippine reaction to the international environment. The international economy may set the boundaries within which any Third World nation is free to maneuver, but domestic political factors determine the precise path of development a nation follows.

In the Philippine case we could blame the failure to develop on

163

Marcos, and this would be in part an accurate explanation of why the Philippines lags so far behind its neighbors in East and Southeast Asia—neighbors it once surpassed in levels of economic development. It would, however, overlook the fact that Marcos existed in a domestic and international political economy of which large parts were beyond his control. Even a powerful authoritarian ruler, using all the coercive and administrative powers that the modern state commands, could not control the international price of commodities, nor could he have maintained his personal power while seeking to lessen the nation's external dependence on and interaction with the U.S. military or the IMF/World Bank group. In the end Marcos was unable to guarantee even his own independence from societal demands, and he was driven from office by a multi-class coalition that opposed his continued rule.

Now the regime has changed, but has the Philippine state also changed? I believe it has changed, but very little. The cronies are gone and the state capitalists have been weakened; therefore the Aquino government must defend and enhance the interests of essentially the same state as when Marcos held political power. This harsh fact determines the narrow limits within which the Aquino government and all subsequent governments will find themselves constrained. Change, if it is to have a significant impact on the lives of the millions of Filipinos who produce the agricultural exports of the nation, must come not just at the level of the regime but also at the level of the state.

Appendixes

Appendix 1. Leading agricultural exports, 1970–1979 (volume in metric tons)

Year	Coconut oil	Sugar	Desiccated coconut	Copra	Bananas	Copra meal/cake	Canned pineapple
1970	338,858	1,227,570	67,426	445,073	82,017	231,362	99,980
1971	397,420	1,344,677	72,666	692,464	267,243	288,012	100,488
1972	465,775	1,224,347	75,987	425,640	422,421	351,646	108,106
1973	430,085	1,474,471	78,049	734,431	465,786	263,214	90,923
1974	415,742	1,542,081	63,909	267,697	662,999	270,685	125,307
1975	614,386	972,217	66,245	761,147	822,742	302,962	116,393
1976	862,497	1,466,012	81,003	149,722	796,178	497,632	138,336
1977	769,631	2,441,566	97,952	634,636	692,689	436,112	154,447
1978	1,016,998	1,124,245	90,831	365,241	776,496	534,673	161,636
1979	803,483	1,150,296	85,814	144,743	858,606	548,301	188,609
1980	917,607	1,735,257	87,164	123,258	922,707	530,597	187,019
1981	1,039,900	1,222,041	86,337	106,385	868,556	633,110	173,500
1982	921,237	1,247,520	90,251	191,788	926,684	589,572	170,862
1983	998,252	962,761	89,362	12,325	643,375	616,712	145,705
1984	587,757	877,183	76,618	0	799,649	375,610	170,940

SOURCE. Central Bank of the Philippines, *Statistical Bulletin 1979* and *Statistical Bulletin 1984* (Manila, 1980 and 1985).

Appendix II. Philippine coconut oil mills, proposed and existing (as of 1978)

Name	Daily rated capacity (copra metric tons)	BOI approved	UNICOM takeover
Granexport Mfg.	1000	*	*
Legaspi Oil Mills	1000		*
Lu Do and Lu Ym Corp.	900	*	*
San Pable Mfg. Corp.	450		*
Southern Islands Oil Mill	400	*	*
Cagayan de Oro Oil Co.	350	*	*
Imperial Vegetable Oil Co.	310	*	
Davao Gulf Oil Mill	300	*	
Iligan Coconut Industries	300	*	*
Interco Mfg. Co.	300	*	
Philippine International Development	300		
Philippine Refining Co.	275		
Mindanao Coco Oil Mfg.	250	*	*
Iligan Bay Mfg.	250	*	*
Coco Complex Phils.	250	*	
Coco-Chemical Philippines	250	*	
Proctor and Gamble, PMC	250		
Tantuco Industrial and Development Corp.	240		
Philippine Argo Edible Oil	200	*	*
Lim Ket Kai	200		
Tantuco Enterprises	195		
International Oil Factory	175		
Central Vegetable Oil Co.	150		
Lucena Oil Factory	150		*
Pacific Oil Products	150		
Royal Industrial Dev't Corp.	130		
NIDC Leyte	125		
NIDC Davao	125		
NIDC Jimenez	125		
Royal Manufacturing Corp.	115		
Orcar Corp.	110	*	
Liberty Oil Factory	100		
Metroplex Commodities	100		
PCY Oil Mfg. Corp.	100		*
West Visayas Coco Development	100	*	
Fifteen small oil mills operating without BOI incentives and not taken over			
Total BOI approved	4,970		
Total non-BOI approved	5,397		
Grand total existing	10,367		
Proposed Mills			
Olasahar Oil Mills	250	*	*
Surigao Coconut Dev't. Corp.	250	*	*
Cebu Coconut Processing	250	*	

(*continued*)

Appendix II. (Continued)

Name	Daily rated capacity (copra metric tons)	BOI approved	UNICOM takeover
Southern Leyte Oil Mill	250	*	*
Noroil Oil Mills	250	*	*
People's Industrial	250	*	
Muslim Integrated	250		
Maguindanao Integrated	200	*	
Mindoro Agro Mfg.	100	*	
Samarland Coconut Products	100	*	
Sarranganni Bay Coco Oil	100	*	
Coco Resources	50		*
Languna Insular Commercial	50		
Bicol Oil Mill and Refinery	50		
Proposed Total	2,900		
Grand total—existing and proposed	13,267		

SOURCE. Philippine Coconut Oil Producers Association, "A Matter of Concern: The Coconut Oil Business," mimeo. (Manila: n.d.).

Appendix III. Exports of copra and coconut oil, 1899–1940 (metric tons)

Year	Copra exports	Percent value of all exports	Coconut oil exports	Percent value of all exports
1899	15,353	5%	—	—
1900	64,891	14	—	—
1901	32,518	7	—	—
1902	59,227	9	3	—
1903	82,154	12	1	—
1904	38,572	7	—	—
1905	55,749	10	10	—
1906	60,586	13	654	—
1907	58,622	14	820	—
1908	97,495	19	2,852	1%
1909	109,033	22	—	—
1910	120,484	26	—	—
1911	142,148	29	—	—
1912	142,793	26	1	—
1913	82,219	20	5,010	2
1914	87,345	16	11,914	5
1915	139,093	21	13,464	5
1916	72,277	10	16,091	6
1917	92,180	9	45,198	12
1918	55,062	4	115,281	23
1919	25,094	4	139,943	33
1920	25,083	2	77,571	15
1921	150,335	15	90,292	18
1922	173,052	15	107,208	16
1923	207,131	16	89,183	12
1924	156,762	12	111,629	13
1925	146,709	11	104,128	14
1926	174,021	14	117,291	16
1927	199,319	12	144,803	16
1928	234,417	15	142,243	15
1929	173,573	9	190,519	18
1930	174,300	10	147,365	14
1931	174,239	8	164,970	14
1932	137,241	5	114,673	8
1933	208,753	8	159,621	9
1934	342,706	8	144,836	6
1935	252,900	12	169,194	13
1936	291,088	11	159,623	10
1937	236,544	11	163,297	14
1938	342,067	11	165,623	9
1939	400,667	8	164,724	—
1940	341,930	6	177,459	—

SOURCE. U.S. House, Committee on Insular Affairs, *To Provide for the Rehabilitation of the Philippine Islands, Appendix to Hearings,* 79th Cong., 2d sess. (1946), Tables 25 and 28.

Appendix IV. Coconut exports, 1949–1978 (value in U.S. $ thousand, quantity in thousand kilograms)

Year	Total value of exports	Copra exports		Desiccated coconut		Coconut oil	
		Quantity	Value	Quantity	Value	Quantity	Value
1949	247,854	528,747	89,643	57,637	19,366	61,304	17,510
1950	331,035	707,186	137,953	73,050	24,157	69,086	12,482
1951	427,447	775,026	153,131	47,452	14,902	77,854	24,496
1952	345,727	670,843	90,670	39,081	9,740	80,548	15,421
1953	398,252	606,694	116,976	49,496	15,748	59,473	17,144
1954	400,504	763,230	130,075	45,659	13,524	65,208	16,568
1955	400,649	804,838	118,680	48,529	12,810	74,177	16,535
1956	453,179	966,303	134,100	48,691	12,858	108,929	23,976
1957	431,062	943,100	131,958	54,935	15,153	97,646	21,356
1958	492,758	811,878	139,079	51,631	16,410	86,956	24,091
1959	529,493	681,107	138,073	49,499	18,166	64,629	22,484
1960	560,389	804,371	138,643	58,775	18,837	59,695	15,669
1961	499,512	627,532	88,196	59,150	14,529	74,378	15,939
1962	556,021	779,441	112,955	62,584	15,070	147,603	31,570
1963	727,106	1,032,660	168,259	70,297	18,405	195,321	46,714
1964	742,036	910,019	156,091	69,524	19,524	229,447	59,936
1965	768,448	883,495	170,004	67,730	20,447	235,759	68,095
1966	828,195	940,386	157,163	67,161	17,713	309,649	74,509
1967	821,456	775,189	129,435	60,878	17,046	230,290	59,274
1968	926,114	706,908	135,875	78,875	30,712	267,088	80,474
1969	983,173	575,822	98,330	52,277	15,625	212,528	53,915
1970	1,142,191	447,443	80,581	66,241	18,083	339,241	97,567
1971	1,136,431	692,464	114,040	72,666	20,741	397,420	103,451
1972	1,105,538	925,640	110,480	75,987	17,551	465,775	84,269
1973	1,837,188	734,431	165,764	78,049	32,456	427,373	151,083
1974	2,724,989	267,697	139,784	63,909	60,300	415,120	380,020
1975	2,294,470	761,147	172,318	66,245	30,429	614,387	230,299
1976	2,573,676	822,736	149,722	81,003	37,494	862,497	298,713
1977	3,150,887	634,636	200,525	97,952	90,047	769,631	412,237
1978	3,424,876	365,241	135,684	90,831	81,888	1,016,998	620,572

SOURCE. United Coconut Association of the Philippines, *Coconut Statistics, 1979* (Manila, 1979).

Year est.	Sugar central	Province	Initial daily capacity (metric tons)
1909	St. Louis Oriental Factory/Hind Sugar Co.	Pangasinan	300
1910	Philippine Milling Co.	Mindoro	1,550
1912	San Isidro	Negros	110
1912	Santa Aniceta	Negros	400
1914	Calamba Sugar estate	Laguna	5,000
1914	Central Azucarera de Caletegan	Batangas	772
1914	Philippine Sugar Estate Development Co.		750
1914	San Carlos Milling Co., Inc.	Negros Occ.	2,625
1915	Kabankalan Sugar Co., Inc.	Negros Occ.	850
1916	Central Palma	Negros	600
1917	Central San Isidro	Negros	680
1918	North Negros Sugar Co., Inc./ Victorias	Negros Occ.	3,600
1919	Pampanga Sugar Mills/Integrated Sugar Central Co.	Pampanga	4,200
1919	Central Azucarere de Bais	Negros Or.	3,500
1919	Isabela Sugar Co., Inc./Binalbagan-Isabela	Negros	2,480
1920	Bacolod-Murcia Milling Co., Inc.	Negros Occ.	3,500
1920	La Carlota Sugar Central	Negros Occ.	4,306
1920	Ma-ao Sugar Central Co., Inc.	Negros Occ.	3,000
1920	Victorias Milling Co., Inc.	Negros Occ.	2,300
1920	Hawaiian-Philippines Co.	Negros Occ.	3,300
1921	Central Azucarera de Don Pedro	Batangas	2,600
1921	Mabalacat Sugar Development Co., Inc.	Pampanga	256
1921	Pampanga Sugar Development Co., Inc.	Pampanga	4,800
1921	Binalbagan Estate, Inc.	Negros Occ.	3,022
1921	Talisay-Silay Milling Co., Inc.	Negros Occ.	4,000
1921	Asturias Sugar Central	Capiz	1,350
1924	Pilar Sugar Central	Capiz	900
1925	Hind Sugar Co.	Pangasinan	400
1925	Luzon Sugar Co.		500
1927	Bataan Sugar Estate	Bataan	300
1927	Central Azucarera del Danao	Negros	700
1927	Lopez Sugar Central	Negros Occ.	1,000
1927	Nueva Ecija Sugar Mills	Nueva Ecija	331
1928	Central Azucarera de Tarlac	Tarlac	6,000
1928	Mt. Arayat Sugar Co., Inc.	Pampanga	1,000
1928	Central Sara-Ajuy	Panay	750
1928	Cebu Sugar Co., Inc./Bogo-Medellin	Cebu	1,000
1929	Panique Sugar Mills, Inc.	Tarlac	816
1929	Central Santos-Lopez	Iloilo	1,000
1929	Bogo-Medellin Milling Co., Inc.	Cebu	1,000
1929	Ormoc-Rosario	Leyte	800
1930	Central Azucarera del Norte	Ilocos Norte	450
1930	Central Leonor	Negros	400
1930	Central Lourdes	Panay	220
1930	Philippine Starch and Sugar Co.	Panay	850

SOURCES. Republic of the Philippines, National Wage Commission, *The 1977 Sugar Industry Study* (Manila, n.d.); Philippine Sugar Institute, *Statistical Series on Sugar* 5, no. 1 (January 1975); and Carlos Quirino, *History of the Philippine Sugar Industry* (Manila: Kalayaan, 1974).

Appendix VI. Sugar centrals established since World War II

Year est.	Sugar Central	Province	Initial daily capacity (metric tons)
1962	Agro-Industrial Dev't of Silay-Sarabia	Negros Occ.	3,000
1963	First Farmers Milling Co.	Negros Occ.	3,500
1969	Sagay Sugar Central Inc.	Negros Occ.	4,000
1969	Batangas Sugar Central	Batangas	4,000
1970	Southern Negros Sugar Central	Negros Occ.	4,000
1970	Passi Sugar Central	Iloilo	4,000
1970	Durano and Co.	Cebu	2,000
1970	Calinog-Lambunao Sugar Mill	Iloilo	4,000
1970	Central Azucarera y Refineria de Bataan, Inc.	Bataan	3,000
1970	New Frontier Sugar Corp.	Iloilo	4,000
1971	Talong Sugar Central	Negros Or.	3,000
1971	Dacongcogon Sugar Central	Negros Occ.	1,500
1971	Davao Sugar Central	Davao	4,000
1972	Hilongos Development Co., Inc.	Leyte	5,000
1974	Bicol Sugar Development Co.	Camarines S.	4,000
1976	United Sugar Milling Co.	Negros Or.	4,000
1976	Bukidnon Sugar Milling Co.	Bukidnon	4,000
1977	Cagayan Sugar Co.	Cagayan	4,000
1977	North Cotabato Sugar Industry, Inc.	N. Cotabato	4,000

SOURCES. Republic of the Philippines, National Wage Commission, *The 1977 Sugar Industry Study* (Manila, n.d.); Philippine Sugar Institute, *Statistical Series on Sugar* 5, no. 1 (January 1975); and Carlos Quirino, *History of the Philippine Sugar Industry* (Manila: Kalayaan, 1974).

Appendix VII. Philippine sugar production—centrifugal, muscovado, and panocha (in short tons)

Year	Total production	Centrifugal	% total	Total muscovado & panocha	% total
1920	466,912	91,060	20%	375,852	80%
1921	589,437	293,132	34	386,305	66
1922	533,189	217,943	41	315,246	59
1923	475,325	258,763	54	216,562	46
1924	529,091	325,046	61	204,045	39
1925	779,510	551,621	71	227,889	29
1926	607,362	407,703	67	199,659	33
1927	766,902	586,833	77	180,069	23
1928	807,814	634,585	79	173,229	21
1929	933,955	769,394	82	164,561	18
1930	983,767	866,913	88	116,854	12
1931	958,032	871,297	91	86,735	9
1932	1,174,311	1,100,214	94	74,079	6
1933	1,342,795	1,284,986	96	57,809	4
1934	1,652,953	1,597,949	97	54,644	3
1935	754,721	700,311	93	54,410	7
1936	1,042,630	978,865	94	63,765	6
1937	1,186,184	1,117,817	94	68,367	6
1938	1,115,574	1,054,631	95	60,943	5
1939	1,149,376	1,099,510	95	60,866	5
1940	1,141,841	1,049,015	92	92,826	8

SOURCE. U.S. House, Committee on Insular Affairs, *To Provide for the Rehabilitation of the Philippines, Annex to Hearings,* 79th Cong., 2d sess. (1946), 240.

Appendix VIII. Volume and value of Philippine sugar exports, 1920–1940 (quantity in metric tons, value in $U.S. thousands)

Year	To all countries			To United States		
	Quantity	Value	% value of total exports	Quantity	Value	% value of total sugar exports
1920	180,341	49,619	33%	123,937	39,348	79%
1921	289,876	25,518	29	150,479	16,876	66
1922	362,072	25,582	27	244,852	20,010	78
1923	271,983	34,519	29	230,555	30,377	88
1924	357,830	41,868	31	300,867	38,749	89
1925	546,832	45,514	30	463,989	41,416	91
1926	411,232	32,229	24	341,306	29,162	91
1927	553,324	50,296	32	508,317	47,886	95
1928	569,938	47,542	31	534,229	45,691	96
1929	695,868	53,244	32	670,953	52,153	98
1930	743,980	52,240	39	737,195	52,038	99
1931	752,932	49,926	48	752,284	49,944	99
1932	1,016,568	59,801	62	1,016,266	59,792	99
1933	1,078,653	64,333	61	1,078,595	64,328	99
1934	1,152,841	65,454	59	1,152,679	65,444	99
1935	516,233	32,990	35	515,377	32,949	99
1936	899,838	61,937	45	899,615	61,927	99
1937	871,045	57,706	38	868,008	57,610	99
1938	868,253	50,022	43	867,938	50,002	99
1939	874,728	49,673	32	874,728	49,673	100
1940	976,474	47,243	30	976,471	47,243	100

Source. U.S. House Committee on Insular Affairs, *To Provide for the Rehabilitation of the Philippines, Annex to Hearings,* 79th Cong., 2d sess. (1946), 237.

Appendix IX. Philippine Sugar Production, 1934–1979

Crop year	Number of mills operating	Area planted	Production (thousands of short tons)	Yield (metric tons/hectare)
1934–35	46	283,269	1,578	45.41
45–46	5	2,390	13	43.06
46–47	16	15,236	85	43.75
47–48	23	74,444	398	43.75
48–49	27	117,504	729	47.47
49–50	28	127,903	685	43.01
50–51	27	154,607	935	47.98
51–52	28	188,503	1,077	47.98
52–53	25	209,265	1,134	45.29
53–54	25	220,596	1,434	53.62
54–55	25	218,443	1,372	51.98
55–56	25	188,015	1,219	52.45
56–57	25	178,006	1,143	50.66
57–58	25	183,700	1,378	57.86
58–59	24	193,822	1,512	62.03
59–60	24	206,762	1,529	62.04
60–61	24	210,075	1,415	55.91
61–62	25	216,484	1,618	60.46
62–63	25	264,336	1,714	57.76
63–64	25	282,410	1,856	48.22
64–65	27	327,610	1,717	49.75
65–66	26	297,516	1,545	44.64
66–67	26	287,949	1,720	53.06
67–68	26	305,810	1,760	50.73
68–69	27	319,447	1,761	51.49
69–70	33	346,393	2,124	61.89
70–71	35	407,297	2,270	49.20
71–72	36	420,340	2,003	46.31
72–73	37	434,733	2,476	52.08
73–74	37	468,263	2,696	55.70
74–75	38	513,552	2,638	47.89
75–76	38	544,579	2,875 (MT)	
76–77	40	523,784	2,671 (MT)	
77–78	41	503,425	2,335 (MT)	
78–79	42	429,394	2,287 (MT)	

SOURCES. Republic of the Philippines, National Wage Commission, *The 1977 Sugar Industry Study* (Manila, n.d.), 80–81; Private Development Corporation of the Philippines, *The Sugar Industry* (Manila, 1980), Table 9; and Central Bank of the Philippines, *Statistical Bulletin, 1979* (Manila, 1980), 233.

Notes

CHAPTER 1. *Creation of the Philippine Political Economy*

1. Proclamation No. 1081 is reprinted in Alejandro M. Fernandez, *The Philippines and the United States: The Forging of New Relations* (Quezon City: NSDB-UP Integrated Research Program, 1977).

2. See Walden Bello, David Kinley, and Elaine Elinson, *Development Debacle: The World Bank in the Philippines* (San Francisco: Institute for Food and Development Policy and Philippine Solidarity Network, 1982), and Robin Broad, "Behind Philippine Policy Making: The Role of the World Bank and International Monetary Fund" (diss., Princeton University, 1983).

3. Stephan Haggard, "The Newly Industrializing Countries and the International System," *World Politics* 38 (January 1986), 343–70.

4. Bruce Cumings, "The Origins and Development of the Northeast Asian Political Economy: Industrial Sectors, Product Cycles, and Political Consequences," *International Organization* 38 (Winter 1984), 1–40.

5. Cf. Cheryl Payer, "Exchange Controls and National Capitalism: The Philippine Experience," *Journal of Contemporary Asia* 3 (1973), 54–69.

6. On the role of foreign merchant houses see Benito Fernandez Legarda, Jr., "Foreign Trade, Economic Change, and Entrepreneurship in the Nineteenth Century Philippines" (diss., Harvard University, 1955), 118, and Norman G. Owen, "Americans in the Abaca Trade: Peele, Hubbell and Co., 1856–75," in Peter Stanley, ed., *Reappraising an Empire: New Perspectives on Philippine-American History* (Cambridge: Harvard University Press, 1984).

7. Leslie E. Bauzon, *Philippine Agrarian Reform, 1880–1965*, Institute of Southeast Asian Studies, Occasional Paper no. 31 (Singapore, June 1975), 1.

8. On the role of the Chinese mestizo see Edgar Wickberg, "The Chinese Mestizo in Philippine History," *Journal of Southeast Asian History* 5 (March 1964), 62–100.

9. The first eleven pages of Bauzon's *Philippine Agrarian Reform* give a precise description of the various ways in which land could be accumulated.

10. Almost 215,000 hectares (a hectare is 2.47 acres). See Dennis Morrow Roth, *The Friar Estates of the Philippines* (Albuquerque: University of New Mexico Press, 1977). Also see his "Church Lands in the Agrarian History of the Tagalog Region," in Alfred W. McCoy and Ed. C. de Jesus, eds., *Philippine Social History: Global Trade and Local Transformations* (Honolulu: University Press of Hawaii, and Quezon City: Ateneo de Manila University Press, 1982).

11. U.S., House, Committee on Insular Affairs, *To Provide for the Rehabilitation of the Philippine Islands, Appendix to Hearings,* on S.1610, 79th Cong., 2d sess., 1946, Tables 15 and 32.

12. For an excellent study of the emergence of an agrarian elite based in the prime sugar-producing providence of Pampanga, see John Larkin, *The Pampangans: Colonial Society in a Philippine Province* (Berkeley: University of California Press, 1972). For evidence of the way Spanish rule helped consolidate the rule of the native elite in one region, for at least a period of time, see Ed. C. de Jesus, "Control and Compromise in the Cagayan Valley," in McCoy and de Jesus, *Philippine Social History.*

13. Prior to this time the term *Filipino* had been used to identify Spaniards born in the Philippine colony. This was to distinguish them from *peninsulares,* the Spaniards born in Spain.

14. Larkin, *The Pampangans,* 126.

15. Theodore Friend, *Between Two Empires* (Manila: Solidaridad, 1969), quoting Earl B. Schwulst, "Report on the Budget and Financial Policies of French Indo-China, Siam, Federated Malay States, and the Netherlands East Indies" (April 1931, Philippine Manuscript Reports, 1931, Bureau of Insular Affairs).

16. Ibid., 6.

17. Carl Landè, *Leaders, Factions, and Parties: The Structure of Philippine Politics,* Yale University Southeast Asia Studies, Monograph Series no. 6 (New Haven, Conn., 1965), 28.

18. Norman G. Owen, ed., *Compadre Colonialism: Studies on the Philippines under American Rule,* University of Michigan Papers on South and Southeast Asia no. 3 (Ann Arbor, 1971), 3–4.

19. See, for example the discussion of Manuel Quezon's early political career and his interaction with the American Harry H. Bandholtz, who was later to become director of the Philippine Constabulary, in Michael

Cullinane, "The Politics of Collaboration," in Stanley, *Reappraising an Empire*, 59–84. Cullinane argues that "through encouragement, advice, assistance, the removal of obstacles, the exchange of favors, and numerous other acts in their behalf, Americans facilitated, even participated in, the ascendance and later the consolidation of the political power of Filipinos at all levels of government" (p. 63).

20. Despite their differences over the nature and extent of collaboration with the Japanese, both David Joel Steinberg and Alfred W. McCoy agree that the elite survived the war with political and economic power undiminished. See Steinberg, *Philippine Collaboration in World War II* (Manila: Solidaridad, 1967), and McCoy, ed., *Southeast Asia under Japanese Occupation*, Yale University Southeast Asia Studies Monograph no. 22 (New Haven, 1980).

21. Philippine Trade Act of 1946, Title III, sec. 341, reprinted in Fernandez, *The Philippines and the United States*, A-150–A-177.

22. Corporate Information Center, *The Philippines: American Corporations, Martial Law, and Development* (New York: IDOC-North America, 1973), 9.

23. John Power and Gerardo Sicat, *The Philippines: Industrialization and Trade Policies* (New York: Oxford University Press, 1971), 31–32.

24. Cumings, "Northeast Asian Political Economy," 3, emphases added.

25. Alice H. Amsden, "The State and Taiwan's Economic Development," in Peter Evans, Dietrich Rueschemeyer, and Theda Skocpol, eds., *Bringing the State Back In* (Cambridge: Cambridge University Press, 1985), 81.

26. Peter Evans, *Dependent Development: The Alliance of Multinational, State, and Local Capital in Brazil* (Princeton: Princeton University Press, 1979), 59, 63.

27. Amsden, "The State and Taiwan's Economic Development," 79.

28. See, for example, "NSSD: U.S. Policy towards the Philippines: Executive Summary" (prepared by the National Security Council, leaked by State Dept. employees, and released March 12, 1985, by the Philippine Support Committee), and U.S. Senate, "The Philippines: A Situation Report," Staff Report to the Select Committee on Intelligence (Washington, D.C., November 1, 1985).

29. Robert Baldwin, *Foreign Trade Regimes and Economic Development: The Philippines* (New York: Columbia University Press, 1975), 149.

30. Russell Cheetham and Edward Hawkins, *The Philippines: Priorities and Prospects for Development* (Washington, D.C.: World Bank, 1976), 114.

31. Payer, "Exchange Controls and National Capitalism," 54–69.

32. Robert B. Stauffer, *The Philippine Congress: Causes of Structural Change* (Beverley Hills: Sage, 1975).

33. Kit G. Machado, "Changing Patterns of Leadership Recruitment and the Emergence of the Professional Politician in Philippine Local Politics," in Benedict J. Kerkvliet, ed., *Political Change in the Philippines: Studies of Local Politics Preceding Martial Law* (Honolulu: University Press of Hawaii, 1974), and "Continuity and Change in Philippine Factionalism," in Frank P. Belloni and Dennis C. Beller, eds., *Faction Politics: Political Parties and Factionalism in Comparative Perspective* (Santa Barbara, Calif.: ABC-Clio, 1978), 193–217.

34. Frank H. Golay, *The Philippines: National Policy and National Economic Development* (Ithaca: Cornell University Press, 1961), especially chap. 14, "Economic Nationalism."

35. Jonathon Fast, "Imperialism and Bourgeois Dictatorship in the Philippines," *New Left Review* no. 78 (March–April 1973), 93; Jeffrey Race, *Whither the Philippines?* (n.p.: Institute of Current World Affairs, 1975), 2; and David Wurfel, "Elites of Wealth and Elites of Power, the Changing Dynamic: A Philippine Case Study," *Southeast Asian Affairs, 1979* (Singapore: Institute of Southeast Asian Studies, 1980), 233.

36. As Minister of Industry Vicente Paterno said, "although in the past there have been expressions of the desire to attract foreign investments into the Philippine economy, they were negated by other statements in Congress and in the Constitutional Convention proposing to make changes in the law of the land to impose further restrictions on foreign investment." Paterno, "The BOI: Its Role in the Philippine Industrial Development," *Philippine Quarterly,* June 1973, p. 27, as quoted in Bello, Kinley, and Elinson, *Development Debacle,* 138.

37. Cumings, "Northeast Asian Political Economy," 27.

38. Amsden, "The State and Taiwan's Economic Development," 94.

39. Cheetham and Hawkins, *The Philippines: Priorities and Prospects,* 12.

40. Board of Investments, *Annual Report, 1978* (Manila, 1979). During these years the exchange rate was seven pesos to the U.S. dollar.

41. Kit G. Machado, "Philippine Politics: Research 1960–1980, Areas for Future Explanation," in Donn V. Hart, ed., *Philippine Studies: Political Science, Economics and Linguistics,* Northern Illinois University Center for Southeast Asian Studies, Occasional Paper no. 8 (DeKalb, 1981).

42. Landé, *Leaders, Factions, and Parties,* 123.

43. Jean Grossholtz, *Politics in the Philippines* (Boston: Little, Brown, 1964), and Machado, "Philippine Politics: Research 1960–1980," 3–4.

44. Landé, *Leaders, Factions, and Parties,* 78. Landé goes on to say that "like the English gentry of earlier centuries, these middle-level leaders scattered throughout the countryside have sufficient personal wealth to maintain their own large followings among the electorate and thus to risk

the withholding of government patronage which temporary defiance of the national leadership might entail" (pp. 78–79).

45. Kit G. Machado, "From Traditional Faction to Machine: Changing Patterns of Political Leadership and Organization in the Rural Philippines," *Journal of Asian Studies* 33 (August 1974), 523–47.

46. Thomas C. Nowak and Kay A. Snyder, "Clientelist Politics in the Philippines: Integration or Instability?" *American Political Science Review* 68 (September 1974), 1147. Also see their "Economic Concentration and Political Change in the Philippines," in Kerkvliet, *Political Change in the Philippines,* 153–241.

47. Machado, "From Traditional Faction," 546, and Nowak and Snyder, "Clientelist Politics in the Philippines," 1148.

48. O'Donnell's arguments are presented in his *Modernization and Bureaucratic-Authoritarianism: Studies in South American Politics,* University of California Institute for International Studies, Politics of Modernization Series no. 9 (Berkeley, 1973), and his case study of Argentina, "State and Alliances in Argentina, 1956–1976," *Journal of Development Studies* 15 (October 1978), 3–23. The O'Donnell thesis is also of central concern in the collection edited by David Collier, *The New Authoritarianism in Latin America* (Princeton: Princeton University Press, 1979).

49. See Fermin D. Adriano, "A Critique of the Bureaucratic-Authoritarian State Thesis: The Case of the Philippines," *Journal of Contemporary Asia* 14 (1984), 459–84.

50. Republic of the Philippines, *Statistical Bulletin, 1979* (Manila: Central Bank of the Philippines, 1980), 163–64, Table V.10.

51. On labor relations see Elias Ramos, *Philippine Labor in Transition* (Quezon City: New Day, 1976), and Edberto M. Villegas, *Notes on the Labor Code and the Conditions of the Industrial Working Class in the Philippines,* University of the Philippines, Third World Studies, The Philippines in the Third World Papers Series no. 23 (Quezon City, June 1980).

On agrarian reform see Benedict Kerkvliet, "Land Reform or Counterinsurgency?" in David Rosenberg, ed., *Marcos and Martial Law in the Philippines* (Ithaca: Cornell University Press, 1979), 113–44; Joel Rocamora and David O'Connor, "The U.S., Land Reform, and Rural Development in the Philippines," in Walden Bello and Serverina Rivera, eds., *The Logistics of Repression* (Washington, D.C.: Friends of the Filipino People, 1977), 63–92; and Linda Richter, *Land Reform and Tourism Development in the Philippines* (Cambridge, Mass.: Schenkman, 1982).

On government-media relations see David Rosenberg, "Liberty versus Loyalty: The Transformation of Philippine News Media under Martial Law," in Rosenberg, *Marcos and Martial Law in the Philippines,* 145–79; Gerald Sussman, *Telecommunication Transfers: Transnational Corporations, the*

Philippines and Structures of Domination, University of the Philippines, Third World Studies Program Dependency Papers Series no. 35 (Quezon City, June 1981); and Robert Youngblood, "Government-Media Relations in the Philippines," *Asian Survey* 21 (1981), 710–28.

On government-church relations see Robert Youngblood, "The Protestant Church in the Philippines New Society," *Bulletin of Concerned Asian Scholars* 12 (October 1979), 19–29, and "Structural Imperialism: An Analysis of the Catholic Bishops' Conference of the Philippines," *Comparative Political Studies* 15 (April 1982), 29–56.

Representative of the voluminous documentation on these issues are *Report of an Amnesty International Mission to the Republic of the Philippines, November 1980* (London, 1982); *Pumipiglas—Political Detention and Military Atrocities in the Philippines* (Manila: Association of Major Religious Superiors in the Philippines, Task Force Detainees Philippines, 1980); *Iron Hand, Velvet Glove: Studies on Militarization in Five Critical Areas in the Philippines* (Geneva: World Council of Churches, 1980); Leo Gonzaga, "The Country Comes First: New Curbs on the Philippine Union Movement Are Justified on the Grounds of National Interest," *Far Eastern Economic Review,* September 24, 1982, p. 110; Enrico Paglaban, "Philippines: Workers in the Export Industry," *Pacific Research* 9 (March–June 1978); William Butler, John Humphrey, and G. E. Bisson, *The Decline of Democracy in the Philippines* (Geneva: International Commission of Jurists, 1977); and Sheila Ocampo, "A Little Vietnam: Faced with an Intense Communist Insurgency in the South, Manila Tries an Indochina War Style Strategic Hamlet Programme," *Far Eastern Economic Review,* March 12, 1982, p. 38.

52. Robert Stauffer, "The Political Economy of Refeudalization," in Rosenberg, *Marcos and Martial Law in the Philippines,* 180–218; Vivencio Jose, ed., *Mortgaging the Future: The World Bank and IMF in the Philippines* (Quezon City: Foundation for Nationalist Studies, 1982); Bello, Kinley, and Elinson, *Development Debacle;* and Broad, "Behind Philippine Policy Making."

53. See the review essay by Mark W. Turner, "The Political Economy of the Philippines: Critical Perspectives," *Pacific Affairs* 57 (Fall 1984), 462–70.

54. Fernando Henrique Cardoso, "On the Characterization of Authoritarian Regimes in Latin America," in Collier, *The New Authoritarianism in Latin America,* 51, 50.

55. Raymond Duvall and John Freeman, "The State and Dependent Capitalism," *International Studies Quarterly* 25 (March 1981), 106; O'Donnell, "State and Alliances in Argentina, 1956–76," 24; and Fernando Henrique Cardoso and Enzo Faletto, *Dependence and Development in Latin America* (Berkeley: University of California Press, 1979), 52.

56. See Alfred Stepan, *The State and Society: Peru in Comparative Perspective* (Princeton: Princeton University Press, 1978), chap. 1, for a discussion of "liberal-pluralist, classic Marxist, and organic-statist approaches to the state."

57. David Becker, *The New Bourgeoisie and the Limits of Dependency: Mining, Class, and Power in "Revolutionary" Peru* (Princeton: Princeton University Press, 1983), 6.

58. Robert Snow, *The Bourgeois Opposition to Export Oriented Industrialization in the Philippines*, University of the Philippines, Third World Studies, the Philippines in the Third World Papers Series no. 39 (Quezon City, October 1983).

59. Theda Skocpol, *States and Social Revolutions: A Comparative Analysis of France, Russia, and China* (Cambridge: Cambridge University Press, 1979), 29.

60. O'Donnell, "State and Alliance in Argentina, 1956–1976," 24.

CHAPTER 2. *The Coconut Industry*

1. Republic of the Philippines, National Economic and Development Authority, *1980 Philippine Statistical Yearbook* (Manila, 1980), Tables 5.2 and 12.4.

2. Republic of the Philippines, Philippine Coconut Authority, *The Philippine Coconut Industry* (Quezon City, n.d.), 27.

3. Virgilio David, "The Barriers in the Development of the Philippine Coconut Industry" (thesis, Ateneo de Manila University, 1977), 69.

4. Republic of the Philippines, Ministry of Agriculture, Special Studies Division, *Coconut Socio-Economic and Marketing Survey Philippines*, by A. M. Valiente, Jr., et al. (Quezon City: Ministry of Agriculture, 1979). Information presented in this section is drawn from this survey unless otherwise noted.

5. Gelia T. Castillo, *Beyond Manila: Philippine Rural Problems in Perspective* (Ottawa: International Development Research Centre, 1979), 51.

6. Ibid.

7. Republic of the Philippines, National Science Development Board, Food and Nutrition Research Institute, *First Nationwide Nutrition Survey Philippines, 1978*, FNRI Publication no. GP-11 (Manila: FNRI, 1979), vi, 27.

8. Republic of the Philippines, National Census and Statistics Office, "Coco in a Nutshell," *Journal of Philippine Statistics* 27 (First Quarter, 1976), ix, and Ministry of Agriculture, *Coconut Socio-Economic and Marketing Survey*, 1.

9. U.S., House, Committee on Insular Affairs, *To Provide for the Rehabilitation of the Philippine Islands, Appendix to Hearings,* on S.1610, 79th Cong., 2d sess., 1946, p. 248.

10. Private Development Corporation of the Philippines, *The Coconut Oil Milling Industry* (Manila, 1978), 4.

11. House Committee on Insular Affairs, *Appendix to Hearings,* 251.

12. George L. Hicks, *The Philippine Coconut Industry: Growth and Change, 1900–1965,* Field Report no. 17 (Washington, D.C.: National Planning Association, 1967), 56.

13. United Coconut Association of the Philippines, *Coconut Statistics, 1979* (Manila, 1979), 177.

14. Private Development Corporation of the Philippines, *Coconut Oil Milling Industry,* 5–6, and United Coconut Association of the Philippines, *Coconut Statistics, 1979,* p. 128.

15. United Coconut Association of the Philippines, *Coconut Statistics, 1979,* p. 129.

16. Philippine Coconut Oil Producers Association, "A Matter of Concern, The Coconut Oil Business," mimeo. (Manila, n.d.), 2–3.

17. *Business Day,* January 6, 1977, and February 22, 1977.

18. Republic of the Philippines, National Economic and Development Authority, *Five-Year Philippine Development Plan, 1978–82* (Manila, 1977), 117.

19. Philippine Coconut Producers Federation (COCOFED), "The Legal Personality of COCOFED," mimeo. (Manila, n.d.), 1. For an examination of the socioeconomic leadership of COCOFED, see David, "Barriers in the Development," chap. 5.

20. *Business Day,* January 18, 1980, p. 3.

21. *Business Day,* September 1, 1980, p. 3.

22. *Bulletin Today,* June 6, 1979, p. 24.

23. See *Business Day,* February 8, 1980.

24. Interview with Enrique Zobel, Makati Stock Exchange Building, January 22, 1981.

25. This was the position taken by, among others, A. Gordon Westly, a former official of Jardine Davies, in an interview, Makati, April 7, 1980.

26. Interview with Emmeline Quiño, executive secretary of the National Secretariat of COCOFED, Manila, January 12, 1981.

CHAPTER 3. *The Sugar Industry*

1. For a brief review of some of the public positions taken regarding the sugar workers, see Carlos Quirino, *The History of the Philippine Sugar Industry* (Manila: Kalayaan, 1974).

2. Republic of the Philippines, National Wage Commission, *The 1977 Sugar Industry Study* (Manila, n.d.).

3. *The Sugar Workers of Negros*, a study commissioned by the Association of Major Religious Superiors in the Philippines (Philippines: n.p., n.d.).

4. Ibid., 76–77.

5. John M. Meenahan, "When Sweetness Goes," *Veritas*, October 27, 1985, p. 17.

6. *Business Day*, June 16, 1986, p. 9.

7. U.S., House, Committee on Insular Affairs, *To Provide for the Rehabilitation of the Philippines, Annex to Hearings*, on S.1610, 79th Cong., 2d sess., 1946, p. 234.

8. Quirino, *History of the Philippine Sugar Industry*, 55.

9. Theodore Friend, "The Philippine Sugar Industry and the Politics of Independence, 1929–35," *Journal of Asian Studies* 22 (February 1963), 179–92.

10. Ibid., 180–81.

11. Charles O. Houston, Jr., "The Philippine Sugar Industry, 1934–50," *Journal of East Asiatic Studies* 111 (July–October 1954), 370–71.

12. Quirino, *History of the Philippine Sugar Industry*, 79.

13. House Committee on Insular Affairs, *Hearings*, 256.

14. See Vicente B. Valdepeñas and Germelino M. Bautista, *The Emergence of the Philippine Economy* (Manila: Papyrus, 1977), 179.

15. Cf. Vasanthi Devi Subramanian, "Export Incentives in the Philippines: A Study in Political Dynamics," University of the Philippines Department of Political Science, Discussion Paper no. 80–3 (Manila, 1980).

16. Quoted in Yoshiko Nagano, "The Philippine Sugar Industry in an Export-Oriented Economy: A Thorny Road to Modernization," University of the Philippines Third World Studies, *The Philippines in the Third World Papers* Series no. 12 (Quezon City, 1978), 14.

17. The Taiwan case has been the subject of a great deal of interest of late. One recent example is Thomas Gold, *State and Society in the Taiwan Miracle* (Armonk, N.Y.: M. E. Sharpe, 1986).

18. Comptroller General of the United States, *Foreign Aid Provided through the Operations of the US Sugar Act and the International Coffee Agreement* (Washington, D.C., 1969), 23.

19. This was the position taken by Edgardo Yap, executive officer and secretary treasurer of the Philippine Sugar Association during an interview in Makati, May 5, 1980.

20. These sentiments were widespread, but the specific figures were mentioned by Juan Yulo, a planter and director of La Carlota Sugar Central on October 7, 1980, in Bacolod City; and by Antonio Tianco, director of Sugarcane Research and Extension at Victorias Milling Company, September 30, 1980. Ramon Ponce de Leon, the area vice-president for the

Western Visayas and branch manager of Rizal Commerical Banking Corporation for Bacolod City, was a little more conservative in his estimate. He felt that no less than 50 percent of all planters had been unable to repay their loans and had rolled them over or restructured them. Interview, October 3, 1980, Bacolod City.

21. *Business Day,* June 16, 1986, p. 9.

22. Interview with Eduardo Gamboa, general manager of Philsucom for the Visayas and Mindanao, Bacolod City, October 8, 1980.

23. Interview with Jose Gregorio, director of the Sugarcane Farm Mechanization Program for Philsucom, Bacolod City, October 8, 1980, and memorandum, "Outline of the Philsucom Sugarcane Farm Mechanization Program," from Eduardo Gamboa to Roberto S. Benedicto, November 4, 1979.

24. Interviews, Edgardo Yap, Makati, May 5, 1980, and A. Gordon Westly, Makati, April 7, 1980.

25. Interview, Juan Yulo, Bacolod City, October 7, 1980.

26. Interview, Leonardo Gallardo, former director of the Negros Economic Development Foundation and manager of the Bacolod City office of Atlantic, Gulf and Pacific Company, Bacolod City, October, 1980.

27. Interview, Nigel Rich, executive vice-president, Jardine-Davies, Makati, May 14, 1980.

28. *Bulletin Today,* January 10, 1981, p. 8.

29. Ibid., January 18, 1981, p. 9.

CHAPTER 4. *The Fruit Products Industry*

1. Mark Glago, "American Private Capital in the Philippines, 1898–1941" (thesis, University of Hawaii, 1966), 72, citing a 1964 interview with Calvin Crawford, then president of the Philippine Packing Corporation.

2. Ibid., 73–74.

3. Lorenzo Tañada, *Nationalism: A Summons to Greatness* (Quezon City: Phoenix, 1965), 55.

4. Ibid., 56–57.

5. Ibid., 57–59.

6. Ibid., 59.

7. Interview with Luis Villareal, Agribusiness staff, Ministry of Agriculture, Quezon City, April 14, 1980.

8. Quoted in Vincent G. Cullen, "Sour Pineapples," *America,* November 6, 1976, p. 301.

9. For a description of the PPC expansion based on interviews with many displaced farmers, see Robin Broad, "Our Children Are Being Kid-

napped: The Story of Del Monte's Philippine Packing Corporation in Bukidnon," *Bulletin of Concerned Asian Scholars* 12 (July–September 1980), 2–9.

10. *SEC-Business Day's 1000 Top Corporations in the Philippines* (Quezon City: Business Day Corp., 1980), 128–29.

11. *Honolulu Star-Bulletin,* August 27, 1959, p. 15.

12. Tañada, *Nationalism,* 59–60.

13. Ibid., pp. 60–63.

14. *SEC-Business Day's 1000 Top Corporations,* 128–29.

15. Randolf S. David, "Banana Politics in the Philippines," *ASEAN Business Quarterly,* First Quarter 1981, p. 12.

16. Tañada, *Nationalism,* 160–70.

17. Randolf S. David et al., *Transnational Corporations and the Philippine Banana Export Industry* (Quezon City: Third World Studies Program, University of the Philippines, 1981), 141–42.

18. Ibid., 145.

19. Ibid., 176.

20. Interview, anonymity granted, June 16, 1980, Davao City.

21. During an interview, Roberto Sebastian, field manager for the Marsman Estate Plantations and head of the Growers Bargaining Team with Del Monte, said Floirendo had debts amounting to some three million pesos which were repaid by United Fruits Company at the time they concluded the agreement with TADECO. Interview, Sto. Tomas, Davao del Norte, July 31, 1980.

22. ICL Research Team, *The Human Cost of Bananas* (Manila: n.p., n.d.), 93.

23. David et al., *Transnational Corporations,* 93–95.

24. Ibid., 103–13.

25. Interview, Evelyn Fanlo, secretary for Samahang Magsasaging ng Dabaw (Association of Banana Growers of Davao), July 29, 1980, Davao City.

26. Interview, Roberto Sebastian, July 31, 1980.

27. Interview, Evelyn Fanlo, July 29, 1980.

28. Interview, Roberto Sebastian, July 31, 1980.

29. Quoted in *Business Day,* November 8, 1979, p. 1.

30. Quoted in *Asiaweek,* May 2, 1980, p. 44.

31. Interview, Leslie Philip Matupang, field manager for the NDC-Guthrie joint venture, July 21, 1980, San Francisco, Agusan del Sur, and *Business Day,* February 5, 1980, p. 1.

32. *Bulletin Today,* May 31, 1980, p. 24.

33. Andy McCue, "Philippines' New Palm Oil Venture Could Shape Future Contracts," *Asian Wall Street Journal,* July 25, 1980, p. 11.

34. Sime-Darby Officials Eyeing Expansion of Foothold Here," *Bulletin Today*, July 19, 1980, p. 11.

35. "Boustead, UOB with RP Group?" *Business Day*, July 24, 1980, p. 1.

36. Interviews, Rene Navarette, National Development Company, Manila, March 11, 1980, and Edgardo Tordesillas, vice-chairman of the Board of Investments, Makati, November 12, 1980.

37. Quoted in *Bulletin Today*, June 28, 1980, emphasis added.

38. This information is based on discussions with the parish workers of the San Francisco Catholic Church. The church itself is staffed by Dutch Carmelite missionaries. I shared what information I could gather outside the province about the NGPI project with the missionaries and parish workers, and they in turn shared with me their discussions with settlers. They also asked specific questions of the farmers for me and surveyed the number of families to be affected by the project. After some discussion I accepted their advice that it was best that I, as an outsider and foreigner, not speak directly to the settlers, primarily because the settlers were suspicious of outsiders—they had recently been forced to deal with several trying to convince them to give up their land.

39. According to Leslie Matupang, field manager of NGPI, in an interview, July 21, 1980.

40. Guy Sacerdoti and Sheilah Ocampo, "Guthrie and the Angels," *Far Eastern Economic Review*, November 19, 1982, pp. 58–60.

CHAPTER 5. *State and Regime in the Philippine Context*

1. See "PCGG [Philippine Commission on Good Government] Lists Frozen Properties of Kokoy [Benjamin Romualdez]," *Manila Chronicle*, September 21, 1986, p. 2.

2. Interview, Hermenegildo Zayco, Makati, Metro Manila, May 9, 1980.

3. Quotations from Eduardo Lachica, "Bank Criticizes War on Poverty in Philippines," *Asian Wall Street Journal*, January 16, 1981, p. 1.

4. United States Agency for International Development, Mission to the Republic of the Philippines, *Country Development Strategy Statement, Fiscal Year 1982, Philippines* (Manila: USAID, 1980), 27–28.

5. E. S. Browning, "Philippine Communist Guerrillas Gain Strength as Rural Discontent Grows," *Asian Wall Street Weekly*, July 18, 1983, p. 13.

6. Maurice Zeitlin, W. Lawrence Neuman, and Richard Earl Ratcliff, "Class Segments, Agrarian Property, and Political Leadership in the Capitalist Class of Chile," *American Sociological Review* 41 (December 1976), 1009.

7. E. V. K. Fitzgerald, "The Public Investment Criterion and the Role of the State," *Journal of Development Studies* 13 (July 1977), 369–70.

8. For illustrations of bureaucratic capitalism from within the framework of a model of the "bureaucratic polity," see J. L. S. Girling, *The Bureaucratic Polity in Modernizing Societies: Similarities, Differences and Prospects in the ASEAN Region* (Singapore: Institute of Southeast Asian Studies, 1981).

9. Most of the cronies got their wealth out of the country well before the fall of Marcos. They are now scattered around the globe.

10. Robert Baldwin, *Foreign Trade Regimes and Economic Development: The Philippines* (New York: Columbia University Press, 1975), 18–19. For an elaboration of the events leading up to the imposition of exchange and import controls, see Baldwin, chap. 2, or John Power and Gerardo Sicat, *The Philippines: Industrialization and Trade Policies* (New York: Oxford University Press, 1971), chap. 2.

11. Guy Whitehead, "Philippine American Economic Relations," *Pacific Research and World Empire Telegram* 4 (January–February, 1973), 3, quoting Ferdinand Marcos, "Foreign Investment and Regional Development," *Philippine Economy and Industrial Journal,* November 1972, p. 37.

12. Frank Golay, *The Philippines: Public Policy and National Economic Development* (Ithaca: Cornell University Press, 1961), 169.

13. Baldwin, *Foreign Trade Regimes,* 149.

14. William Ascher, "Political and Administrative Bases for Economic Policy in the Philippines," internal World Bank paper (Washington, D.C.), 3, 8.

15. Robert T. Snow, *The Bourgeois Opposition to Export-Oriented Industrialization in the Philippines,* University of the Philippines, Third World Studies Center, *The Philippines in the Third World Papers* Series no. 39 (Quezon City, October 1983), and Walden Bello, David Kinley, and Elaine Elinson, *Development Debacle: The World Bank in the Philippines* (San Francisco: Institute for Food and Development Policy and Philippine Solidarity Network, 1982), 128–32.

16. Republic of the Philippines, National Economic and Development Authority, *Philippine Yearbook 1983* (Manila, 1983), 667, Table 18.10.

17. Cf. Theda Skocpol, *States and Social Revolutions: A Comparative Analysis of France, Russia, and China* (Cambridge: Cambridge University Press, 1979), 29.

18. James Kurth, "The Political Consequences of the Product Cycle," *International Organization* 33 (Winter 1979), 1–34.

19. Robert O. Keohane, "Hegemonic Leadership and U.S. Foreign Policy in the 'Long Decade' of the 1950s," in William P. Avery and David P.

Rapkin, eds., *America in a Changing World Political Economy* (New York: Longman, 1982), 49–76.

20. The World Bank blueprint is *The Philippines: Priorities and Prospects for Development* (Washington, D.C.: World Bank, 1976).

21. Bello, Kinley, and Elinson, *Development Debacle*, 24, quoting internal World Bank documents.

22. Ibid., 14.

23. William H. Sullivan, "Relocating Bases in the Philippines," *Washington Quarterly* 7 (Spring 1984), 114–19. Sullivan, formerly U.S. ambassador to Manila, has argued that the only "real alternative" tó Subic Naval Base "is to service the Pacific Fleet from the West Coast of the United States and that such a move would be a very expensive option. . . . As for Clark Air Base facilities, it should come as no surprise to learn that they have become more rather than less important to American military planning in recent years."

24. William E. Berry, Jr., "Philippine Domestic Issues Affecting the Retention of American Military Bases" (paper presented at the 1983 Annual Meeting of the Association for Asian Studies), 13.

25. Sullivan, "Relocating Bases in the Philippines," 119.

26. Ferdinand Marcos, *In Search of Alternatives: The Third World in an Age of Crisis* (Metro Manila: National Media Production Center, n.d.), 180, appen. 1.

27. Text of letter from President Carter to Representative Lester L. Wolff, chairman, Subcommittee on Asian and Pacific Affairs, March 21, 1979, reprinted in U.S., House, Committee on Foreign Affairs, Subcommittee on Asian and Pacific Affairs, *Foreign Assistance Legislation for Fiscal Years 1980–81*, Part 4, Hearings and Markup, 96th Cong., 1st sess. (Washington, D.C., 1979), 65.

28. Office of Planning and Budgeting, Bureau for Program and Policy Coordination, Agency for International Development, *US Overseas Loans and Grants and Assistance from International Organizations* (Washington, D.C., n.d.), 77.

29. U.S., Senate, Committee on Foreign Relations, Report to the Chairman, Statistical Data on *Department of Defense Training of Foreign Military Personnel* (Washington, D.C.: General Accounting Office, April 15, 1980), 71.

30. For a more detailed analysis of the military basis for the warm U.S. relationship with Ferdinand Marcos, see my "United States Support for Marcos and the Mounting Pressures for Change," *Contemporary Southeast Asia* 8 (June 1986), 18–36.

31. Fernando Henrique Cardoso and Enzo Faletto, *Dependency and De-*

velopment in Latin America (Berkeley: University of California Press, 1979), 13, 17.

32. For a fruitful application to Asia, see Bruce Cumings, "The Origins and Development of the Northeast Asian Political Economy: Industrial Sectors, Product Cycles, and Political Consequences," *International Organization* 38 (Winter 1984).

33. Peter Evans, *Dependent Development: The Alliance of Multinational, State and Local Capital in Brazil* (Princeton: Princeton University Press, 1979), 218.

34. World Bank, *The Philippines: Priorities and Prospects,* 190.

35. See Guillermo O'Donnell, "Comparative Historical Formations of the State Apparatus and Socio-economic Change in the Third World," *International Social Science Journal* 32 (1980), and "State and Alliance in Argentina, 1956–76," *Journal of Development Studies* 15 (October 1978).

36. Fernando Henrique Cardoso, "On the Characterization of Authoritarian Regimes in Latin America," in David Collier, ed., *The New Authoritarianism in Latin America* (Princeton: Princeton University Press, 1979), 38.

37. *Business Journal,* December 1981, pp. 2 and 4, and January 1982, pp. 6 and 8.

38. "Invitation to American Investors: US Capital, Technology, and Marketing Know-How Needed in Agribusiness, Says Tanco," *AmCham Journal,* March 1979, p. 54.

39. Bello, Kinley, and Elinson, *Development Debacle,* and Robin Broad, "Behind Philippine Policy Making: The Role of the World Bank and International Monetary Fund" (Ph.D. diss., Princeton University, 1983).

40. Cardoso, "On the Characterization of Authoritarian Regimes in Latin America," 34, 48.

41. *NSSD: U.S. Policy towards the Philippines Executive Summary* (prepared by the National Security Council, leaked by State Department employees, and released March 12, 1985, by the Philippine Support Committee).

42. For example, the Communist Party of the Philippines, in a reassessment of its position to boycott the 1986 presidential election, acknowledged that it "did not correctly understand the character and operation of US policy toward the Marcos regime. It overestimated US capacity to impose its subjective will on local politics and misread the US dilemma over the conflicting needs it had to simultaneously attend to. It failed to appreciate the possible effects on US policy of local developments over which the US did not have full control." *Ang Bayan,* May 1986, p. 1.

43. Jose Galang, "Enter Cory Capitalism," *Far Eastern Economic Review,* March 13, 1986, pp. 50–51.

44. Quoted in "Idle Government Lands up for Reform," *Business Day,* June 6, 1986, p. 16.

45. Carol Espiritu, "Government Sells Excess Export Sugar," *Business Day,* June 6, 1986, p. 2.

46. See Tara Singh, "WB Group Offers $300 M for Privatization Program," *Business Day,* May 19, 1986, p. 2.

47. Ibid., and Ramon Isberto, "Sequestration List: 180 Firms," *Business Day,* May 16, 1986, p. 11.

48. Quoted in "Government to Resist Pressures for Total Import Decontrol," *Business Day,* May 21, 1986, p. 2.

Index

Library of Congress Cataloging-in-Publication Data

Hawes, Gary, 1950–
  The Philippine State and the Marcos regime.

  (Cornell studies in political economy)
  Includes index.
    1. Produce trade—Philippines. 2. Sugar trade—Philippines.
3. Coconut industry—Philippines. 4. Fruit trade—Philippines.
5. Agriculture and state—Philippines. I. Title.
HD9016.P52H38   1987   382'.41'09599   86-29237
ISBN 0-8014-2012-1 (alk. paper)